BARBADOS

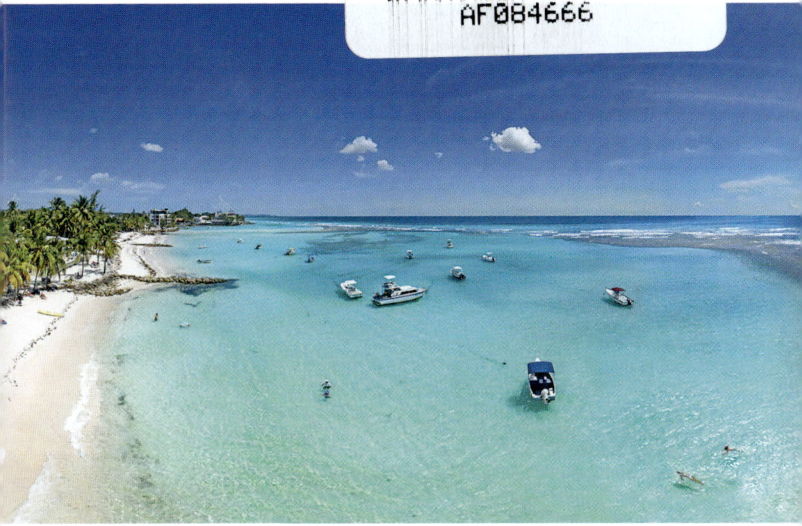

DANIEL AUSTIN & FAEZE SHAD

www.bradtguides.com

Bradt Guides Ltd, UK
The Globe Pequot Press Inc, USA

Bradt GUIDES
TRAVEL TAKEN SERIOUSLY

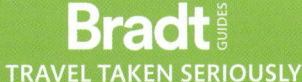

Tourism and Barbados go together like rum and coke or flying fish and chips. You can pay thousands of dollars to be truly cosseted along with music moguls and supermodels, or you can cater for yourself and go shopping with Bajans. The west coast, commonly referred to as the Platinum Coast, is the place to be seen.

The south is for beach life, nightlife, fun and games, the package-holiday end of the market with a cheerful, relaxed atmosphere and the best sand. The Atlantic-facing east coast is a wild, windswept realm of dramatic cliffs, secluded bays and surf-pounded beaches – a paradise for nature lovers and photographers. Head to the hills inland to explore relics of colonial days such as plantation houses, signal towers, tropical gardens, museums and rum distilleries.

Of all the islands in the eastern Caribbean, Barbados is unique in that it remained British throughout its colonial history. Many towns have beautiful parish churches and charming English seaside resort names like Hastings, Brighton or Dover, and the island was often referred to as Little England, a term now laden with heavy colonial baggage.

Since independence in 1966, the country has moved closer in cultural terms to North America while also pursuing its African roots – and in 2021 it became the world's newest republic, marking a bold move to assert its national identity and shed the symbolic ties to the British monarchy. Drum music, once banned by colonial enslavers to prevent slave rebellions, and 'tuk' bands are an essential part of carnival processions. Calypso, soca and steelpan music are a centrepiece of Crop Over, the boisterous festival celebrating the end of the sugar harvest. However, some habits die hard. You can still go to a polo match and be offered tea, or watch Sunday cricket on the village green. A Test Match at the Kensington Oval, though, is a sight to behold – an example of how an English sport has been turned into pure Afro-Caribbean pageantry.

This is **Barbados**

Best of Barbados

top things to do and see

❶ The Garrison Historic Area

If you can tear yourself away from the beach, Bridgetown's Garrison Historic Area is well worth a visit. Dating back to 1650, it's believed to be the most authentic and complete British garrison in the world and was recognized by UNESCO in 2011 for its architectural significance. Watch the changing of the guard, walk through the tunnels or take a tour to find out what George Washington thought about Barbados. Page 37.

❷ Welchman Hall Gully

This is an opportunity to see Barbados' fauna and flora in their natural state; tucked into a ravine, it's a quiet and peaceful haven shaded by tall trees where green monkeys hang out in the canopy while centipedes, frogs and other creatures can be spotted on the forest floor. From the top of the steps there is a wonderful view over much of the island. Page 50.

❸ Flower Forest Botanical Gardens

The best of the island's diverse flora is preserved in this lush tropical forest. Wander among spectacular trees and exotic flowers of all shapes and colours up to the top of the mountain for panoramic views over the wild east coast. It's a wonderfully tranquil place and an oasis of cool on a hot day. Page 52.

④ St Nicholas Abbey

This beautiful plantation house is one of only three genuine Jacobean mansions in the Western Hemisphere and provides a fascinating insight into the history of the sugar trade. In the small working rum distillery you can see sugar cane develop into rum in a traditional pot-still and buy a bottle of the end product, while the quaint Heritage Railway goes through lush gardens to the top of Cherry Tree Hill. Page 58.

⑤ Bathsheba

A jagged arc of golden sand fringed with palm trees, Bathsheba is one of the most stunning beaches on Barbados. Located on the island's undeveloped east coast, it's a wild and windswept place with huge boulders jutting out of the sea. It's not safe for swimming but the huge Atlantic rollers are renowned as a surfers' heaven where young Bajans hone their skills on their boards. Page 63.

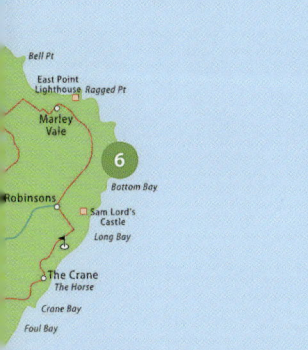

❻ Bottom Bay

Tucked away on the south coast, Bottom Bay is the ultimate tropical beach: a wide expanse of soft pink sand backed with swaying coconut palms and gently lapped by turquoise water. From the high coral cliffs behind the beach there's a panoramic view of the south coast and, if you're lucky, you might spot a turtle or a whale offshore. Page 70.

❼ Oistins Fish Fry

Friday night in Oistins is the island's biggest party. Join the locals as they gather at the bustling seaside fish market with live entertainment, street vendors, crafts and traditional food. Jostle with the crowds and dance the night away with some barbecued flying fish in one hand and a potent rum punch in the other. Page 74.

JOIN

THE TRAVEL CLUB

THE MEMBERSHIP CLUB FOR SERIOUS TRAVELLERS
FROM BRADT GUIDES

Be inspired
Free books and exclusive
insider travel tips
and inspiration

Save money
Special offers and
discounts from our
favourite travel brands

Plan the trip
of a lifetime
Access our exclusive concierge
service and have a bespoke
itinerary created for you
by a Bradt author

Join here:
bradtguides.com/travelclub

Membership levels to suit all budgets

Bradt GUIDES

TRAVEL TAKEN SERIOUSLY

Route planner

putting it all together

Many holidaymakers to the Caribbean only venture out of their all-inclusive resorts on the occasional organized excursion, but, thanks to excellent public transport, good roads and short distances, Barbados is very easy to explore independently. It can take less than an hour to travel from one coast to the next; just a few hours to drive around the entire island, stopping in at one or two tourist attractions and for a leisurely lunch on the way; and, on the highly developed west and south coasts, it's no more than a short walk or bus ride to get to another beach, restaurant or shopping mall. Think of Barbados in five parts. Firstly, there's **Bridgetown** and its environs; while the island's capital is not especially big or appealing, there's good shopping and the **Garrison Historic Area** is interesting to wander around. Secondly, there's the upmarket **west coast**, where the narrow but pretty beaches are lapped by calm waters and lined with luxurious hotels and villas and some superb waterside restaurants. Thirdly, there's the heavily developed **south coast** where the beaches are wider and the sand whiter, and, while the sea is sometimes too rough for safe swimming, the family-friendly resorts have swimming pools and plenty of other amenities for some fun in the sun. Fourthly is the unspoilt, wild, wave-pummelled **east coast**, which has just a few places to stay and eat but makes for scenic driving and hiking with tremendous Atlantic views. Lastly is the island's rolling **interior**, which has a variety of attractions among the sugar cane fields, from plantation houses and rum distilleries to intriguing caves and beautiful flowering botanical gardens.

Best beaches
Paynes Bay Beach, page 44
Bathsheba Beach, page 63
Bottom Bay, page 70
Crane Beach, page 72
Dover Beach, page 75

One to two weeks

If you have only a week to spend on the island, you probably won't want to do much except relax. Take advantage of the beach with a sun lounger, umbrella and rum punch – at your hotel or at one of the many good beach bars. Take a boat trip, go snorkelling with the turtles or dive one of the many colonial-era wrecks littering the seabed. Then in the evening spoil yourself at the plush places

BACKGROUND
The island

Located in the Atlantic Ocean, 483 km north of Venezuela in South America, Barbados is the easternmost island of the Lesser Antilles in the West Indies, and is about 100 km east of the Windward Islands arc and the Caribbean Sea. The island, which is 34 km long, 23 km at its widest point and covers an area of 430 sq km, is sometimes referred to as pear-shaped. The 97 km-long coastline features fine beaches and narrow coastal plains with several steep inland cliffs or ridges. The highest point is Mount Hillaby (340 m) in the north-central area; not a peaked mountain, but an extended ridge about 4 km long. Relatively flat compared to its volcanic neighbours, about 85% of the island is covered by a cap of coral limestone underlain by sedimentary rock up to 600,000 years old. This means that most of the rainwater runs through caves in the limestone – one of these, Harrison's Cave Eco-Adventure Park, has been developed as a tourist attraction – and runs off underground and through steep-sided gullies. The island's water supply is pumped up from the limestone and, as it's filtered, is generally very good for drinking. In the Scotland District in the northeast, the coral limestone has been eroded and older, softer rocks are exposed; the area is made up of clay, sandstone and shale with jutting rocky spikes and ridges. With the exception of the Constitution River in Bridgetown, the island's other three rivers (the Long Pond River and Bruce Vale River in St Andrew, and Joe's River in St Joseph) are in the Scotland District, and have cut deep, steep-sided valleys. Prior to being settled in 1627, Barbados was covered in dense tropical rainforest, but almost all of this was cut down to make way for sugar plantations and later development. Only two examples of this forest remain: Turner's Hall Woods and Joe's River Rain Forest. Barbados was first divided into six parishes in 1629 and later, in 1645, was divided into the present 11 parishes: St Lucy, St Peter, St James, St Thomas, Christ Church, St Michael, St Joseph, St Andrew, St John, St George and St Philip.

with seafront dining on the west or **Platinum Coast** or, if you are on the south coast, wander down to **St Lawrence Gap**, the 'happening' place for restaurants and bars. Other popular options are the dinner and beach party on Mondays and Wednesdays at **Harbour Lights**, and **Oistins Fish Fry** on Fridays with calypso, soca and live music. It's well worth dragging yourself away from the sand to explore the island and put Barbados' history as a British colony into perspective. Hop on a bus to **Bridgetown** one day and spend a morning sightseeing around the **Garrison Historic Area** and along the **Careenage** and shopping along **Broad Street**, with perhaps an afternoon watching cricket at **Kensington Oval**, or rum tasting at the **Mount Gay Visitor Centre**.

Two weeks or more

If you have upwards of a fortnight on Barbados, why not move around a bit? Spend a few days on the south coast first to wind down and enjoy the beach and the nightlife around **St Lawrence Gap**. Then, when the jet lag is behind you and if you can splurge, move up to another resort or plush hotel on the west coast to enjoy some luxury. Finally, stay in a guesthouse on the east coast for a different view of the island: the pounding Atlantic creates a very scenic and wild string of beaches. Hire a car for part of your holiday and tour the island; you can drive all round Barbados in five hours, but there are plenty of interesting places to stop off at on a leisurely tour. You'll also probably get lost, as road signs are not a big feature and the island is criss-crossed with hundreds of little twisty roads through villages. A day on the east coast could be spent at **Bathsheba**, hiking along the old coastal railway, strolling around **Andromeda Botanic Gardens** or lolling about in rock pools. A northern tour could take in **Speightstown**, the **Animal Flower Cave**, **Farley Hill**, the **Barbados Wildlife Reserve** and **Grenade Hall Forest and Signal Station**, **St Nicholas Abbey** and the **Morgan Lewis Sugar Mill**. A day in the middle of the island could encompass **Harrison's Cave Eco-Adventure Park**, **Flower Forest Botanical Gardens**, **Tropical Garden Barbados** and **Gun Hill Signal Station**.

When to go

... and when not to

Climate

With an average of eight to nine hours of daily sunshine and consistently warm sea temperatures, any time of year is holiday time on Barbados. The climate is tropical, but rarely excessively hot because of the prevailing northeast trade winds that gently roll in off the Atlantic. Daytime temperatures average between 28°C and 35°C, the coolest and driest time being December-May, and a wetter and hotter season June-November. Rain is usually heavy when it comes but, because of its easterly position outside the Caribbean Sea basin, Barbados has rarely been hit by hurricanes, although tropical storms may occur August-October.

Festivals

If you want a carnival atmosphere then time your visit for the **Crop Over Festival** (page 16), from late June to early August, a centuries-old tradition that celebrates the end of the sugar cane season. The main carnival celebrations take place on the first weekend of August; book flights, accommodation and car hire in plenty of time for this long weekend as everything is very busy with Barbadians, returning family and friends and visiting tourists. Other musical events worth aiming for are the **Reggae Festival** in April, the **Celtic Festival** in May and the **Jazz Excursion** in October. Cricket lovers should try to take in a **Test Match** or

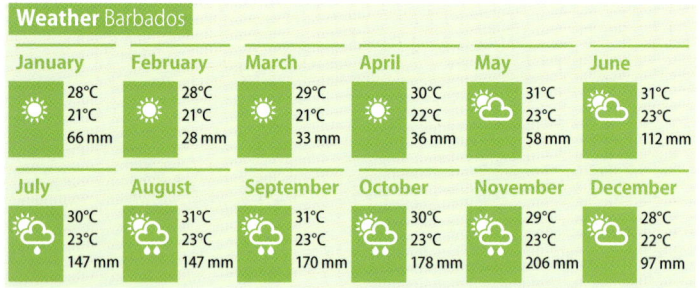

Weather Barbados

Month	High	Low	Rain
January	28°C	21°C	66 mm
February	28°C	21°C	28 mm
March	29°C	21°C	33 mm
April	30°C	22°C	36 mm
May	31°C	23°C	58 mm
June	31°C	23°C	112 mm
July	30°C	23°C	147 mm
August	31°C	23°C	147 mm
September	31°C	23°C	170 mm
October	30°C	23°C	178 mm
November	29°C	23°C	206 mm
December	28°C	22°C	97 mm

a regional competition to see top international players at the Kensington Oval, but there are cricket festivals at other times of the year and of course matches every Sunday in villages around the island. In terms of price, hotel and villa rates are much higher from mid-December to April than at other times of year (especially over Christmas/New Year and Easter, when additional premiums are often charged), while in the quietest and wettest months between September and November, some hotels, restaurants and bars close altogether.

For a diary of events and festivals see www.whatsoninbarbados.com. For public holidays, see page 114.

January

Barbados Horticultural Society (BHS) Annual Flower & Garden Show
BHS Headquarters, Balls Plantation, Christ Church, T428 5889, www.horticulture barbados.com. Held on the last weekend in January, there are lovely floral exhibits from societies affiliated to the BHS including the Barbados Association of Floral Artists, Bonsai Barbados, Barbados Orchid Society and the Barbados Cactus and Succulent Society, as well as craft, tea and food stalls.

February

Holetown Festival *www.holetown festivalbarbados.org.* The week-long festival begins in mid-February and commemorates the first settlers' landing in February 1627. There are parades with floats during the day, all well organized and restrained, nothing outrageous. It features a parade of vintage and classic cars, plus the Queen of the Festival pageant. A few kids march in costume, there are one or two masked performers, and stalls are set up, selling food, Banks beer and crafts. One of the most popular events is the Police Tattoo, a floodlit night show featuring the men and women of the Royal Barbados Police Force. The Police Force band plays on a stage on the beach and the mounted troop, canine unit and motorcycle unit are usually on display. This is Little England par excellence.

Oistins Festival *Bay Gardens, Oistins, Christ Church.* Held over the Easter weekend to celebrate the signing of the Charter of Barbados and the history of this fishing town. There are three days of competitions, parades and demonstrations of fishing skills. Fish-boning is the major competition, the winner being the Queen of the Festival. There are also boat races, the greasy pole and a big street party with live music which goes on until late at night – and of course, lots of fried fish and fishcakes. On Easter Sunday there is a **Gospel Festival**. A very popular event attracting thousands of people.

Best gardens
National Botanical Gardens, page 41
Tropical Garden Barbados, page 42
Flower Forest Botanical Gardens, page 52
Hunte's Gardens, page 52
St Nicholas Abbey, page 58
Andromeda Botanic Gardens, page 64

ON THE ROAD
Flourishing gardens

Barbados has been exhibiting at the UK's prestigious Chelsea Flower Show for almost 40 years and has an impressive 24 gold medals to show for it. The beautiful and creative floral displays are organized by the Barbados Horticultural Society (BHS; T428 5889, www.horticulturebarbados.com), which has been in existence since 1927. A good part of any success at Chelsea comes from mastering the art of transporting flowers and foliage, and each year Team Barbados individually wraps every petal, leaf and stem before boxing them up and dispatching them across the Atlantic to London with British Airways.

In 2019, the new National Botanical Gardens were opened as part of a broader national plan by the government of Barbados to create green spaces for locals and tourists, preserve and showcase native Caribbean flora, and support environmental and conservation goals. In addition to these and other spectacular gardens open to the public on Barbados, such as Tropical Garden Barbados, Hunte's Gardens, Flower Forest Botanical Gardens and Andromeda Botanic Gardens, Barbados has numerous private gardens which are lovingly tended by their owners. Check the events page on the website of the BHS for details of its Open Garden Programme when private gardens can be visited, usually Sundays 1400-1800 in January and February (there is a small entry fee, tea and refreshments). On the last weekend in January, the BHS hosts its Annual Flower and Garden Show at its headquarters at Balls Plantation in Christ Church (once an 18th-century sugar estate), where it has 5 ha (12 acres) of landscaped gardens.

Vujaday Music Festival *www.vujadaymusicfestival.com*. Held over five days in mid-February, this electronic music festival (house, techno, etc) features international DJs, rappers and producers. It's a mobile party at different locations, often on beaches with bars and food vendors.

April
Barbados International Fishing Tournament *Port St Charles, St Peter, https://bgfa.profishingtournaments.com*. Held in mid-April, this, one of the premier fishing events in the southern Caribbean, attracts participants from across the region and internationally for five days of competition. Apart from the fishing, there's much dockside activity and in the evenings people gather to witness the boats arriving with their catch and join in the cocktail parties, a fashion show, wine tasting, live bands, a pig roast and fish fry.
Barbados Reggae Festival *T257 4356, see Facebook*. Held in the third week of April and featuring top-quality local, regional and international reggae acts with a beach party, cruise party and the very popular Reggae on the Hill open-air concert at Farley Hill National Park.

May
Barbados Celtic Festival *T282 7600, see Facebook*. Held over four days at the end of May on the South Coast Boardwalk, this is rather an unusual festival to be celebrated

in the Caribbean, but Barbados attracts Celtic people from around the world for their annual *gymanfa-ganu* and other events including folk music, street theatre, ceilidhs and Celtic chefs. The main event is the Bridgetown Street Parade of marching bands playing pipes and drums on the Saturday afternoon.

Gospelfest *www.barbadosgospelfest.com*. Held over Whitsun, the last weekend in May, this international festival attracts gospel singers from the USA, UK and all over the Caribbean. Concerts are held at various locations including Farley Hill National Park.

June

Sol Rally Barbados *www.rallybarbados. net*. The Caribbean's biggest annual motor sports event started out as a one-day car rally in 1990 and now attracts over 100 international drivers for three days of racing on public roads and off-road routes. There are many vantage points for spectators and several associated social activities.

August

Barbados International Hockey Festival *www.barbadoshockey.org*. Hockey is very popular on Barbados and this is the largest field hockey event in the region, with teams coming from all over the world to participate. Held at Sir Garfield Sobers Sports Complex in late August, matches take place during the day and are followed by beach parties, fêtes, party cruises and clubbing.

October

Barbados Jazz Excursion and Golf Weekend *www.barbadosjazzexcursion. com*. Established in 2014 by Barbados-born soul-jazz saxophonist Elan Trotman, jazz and R&B concerts are held over Columbus Day holiday weekend at the Hilton Barbados Resort and Lighthouse Beach. There's a charity celebrity golf tournament at Apes Hill Club on the Sunday.

November

Independence Day Although the actual day is 30 November, there are several events during the month commemorating Barbados' independence from Britain in 1966, including a parade on the Savannah.

National Independence Festival of Creative Arts (NIFCA) *Contact the National Cultural Foundation, T417 6610, www.ncf.bb*. Plays, concerts and exhibitions in the four weeks before Independence Day on 30 November. Competitors work their way up through parish heats to reach the finals at the Frank Collymore Hall in Bridgetown.

December

Run Barbados Marathon Weekend *www.visitbarbados.org/run-barbados-marathon-weekend*. On the first weekend of December, a full and half marathon, 10 km run and 5 km walk following an 'out and back' mostly flat route, take place from Bridgetown's Bay Street Esplanade, where there's music, family entertainment and food and drink.

ON THE ROAD
Crop Over

The origins of Crop Over, the main festival on Barbados, can be traced back to the 1780s when Barbados was one of the world's largest producers of sugar. For about 30 years around the mid-20th century it went uncelebrated, but was resurrected for tourist purposes in 1974. Since then it has grown into a major celebration of Barbadian culture enjoyed by all, and nobody gets much work done during the six weeks that it lasts – from late June when the sugar cane harvest ends until the first Monday in August: the **Grand Kadooment**. Parades and calypso competitions lead up to this finale, although there are calypso 'tents' and other events during the weeks beforehand.

The celebrations begin with the ceremonial delivery of the last canes on a brightly coloured dray cart pulled by mules, which are blessed. There is a toast to the sugar workers and the crowning of the King and Queen of the crop (the champion cutter-pilers). Weekly calypso tent shows showcase the latest songs with performances by entertainers and comedians as well as calypsonians. Parties, also known as fêtes or bashments, start with after-work liming, hotting up around midnight and going on until daybreak. The **Junior Kadooment Parade** and **Junior Calypso Monarch Competition** give children a chance to have their own carnival and play 'mas'.

Things start to hot up big time on the Friday night preceding the Grand Kadooment with the **Pic-O-De-Crop** semi-finals and **Party Monarch Calypso Competition at Bridgetown's Kensington Oval**. From a line-up of 18, seven competitors are selected to go forward to the finals to compete against the reigning Calypso Monarch.

Following the selection of the King of Pic-O-De-Crop Calypso there is **Fore-Day Morning Jump Up**, an event borrowed from Trinidad's carnival, which is held in the early hours of the Saturday morning. It starts at the National Stadium in Bridgetown and heads out to Mighty Grynner (Spring Garden) Highway; wear old clothes as a lot of oils and paints get liberally smeared around, and it ends with a sunrise beach party. On Sunday night **Cohobblopot** is when the kings and queens of the costume bands show off their creations and compete for prizes and the titles of King and Queen of the Festival. On the Monday, the **Grand Kadooment** is the finale of the carnival, when there is a procession of costume bands through the streets, again along Mighty Grynner (Spring Garden) Highway, accompanied by trucks of deafening sound systems and fuelled by alcohol. Your eyes will be blasted with colour by costumed dancers, stilt walkers and masqueraders, your ears blasted with sound by tuk bands (see box, page 102), calypso, ringbang and steel pan, and your gut blasted by rum, beer, sun, adrenalin and lack of sleep. After the parade the party continues well into the night on Brighton Beach with more revelry, music, food and fireworks.

Details and dates of all events are published on the Barbados Crop Over Festival Facebook page, as well as on the website of Barbados Tourism Marketing Inc (BTMI), www.visitbarbados.org.

What to do

from cricket, golf and polo to diving and sailing

Cricket

Cricket is king on Barbados and everybody has an opinion on the state of the game as well as the latest results. Going to watch a cricket match is an entertaining cultural experience and well worth doing, even if you don't understand the game. Village cricket is played all over the island at weekends; a match here is nothing if not a social occasion. Cricket lovers should try to arrange their visit to coincide with a Test Match or a One Day International at the Kensington Oval (page 30). No sedate Sunday afternoon crowd this – the atmosphere is electric, with DJ music, constant whistling, horn-blowing, cheering and banter. At lunch there are food stalls outside where you can pick up a burger, roti or Bajan stew, buy a T-shirt and West Indies hat and drink a few Banks beers. The biggest crowds come for the matches against England, with touring teams tagging along, but cricket tourists come from as far afield as Australia or South Africa.

Diving and snorkelling

Barbados is surrounded by an inner reef and an outer barrier reef. On the west coast the inner reef is within swimming distance for snorkelling or learning to dive, while the outer reef is a short boat ride away and the water is deeper. Here you can see barracuda, kingfish, moray eels, turtles and squid as well as some fine black coral, barrel sponges and sea-fans. The underwater landscape may not be as pristine as some other islands, but there are some excellent wrecks worth exploring and Carlisle Bay is littered with bottles, cannon balls, anchors and small items such as buckles and buttons after many centuries of visiting ships 'losing' things overboard or sinking. There are 200 reported wrecks in Carlisle Bay, but another popular dive site is the SS *Stavronikita* in the Folkestone Marine Park, one of the best diving wrecks in the Caribbean (page 50). Water temperatures are usually about 25°C in winter and 28°C in summer, with visibility of 15-30 m. A highlight for snorkellers is to swim with the turtles – at Sandy Bay you can see them close to the beach; otherwise Paynes Bay and Folkestone Marine Park offer plenty of opportunity for those prepared to swim out a distance to find them. A number of tour operators run boat excursions to sites frequented by turtles.

Golf

Many keen golfers come to Barbados just to play golf and there are enough courses

ON THE ROAD
Open House Programme

On some Saturdays and Wednesdays between January and April, the Barbados National Trust (T426 2421, www.barbadosnationaltrust.com, see also page 78) organizes public visits to some of the island's most historic and elegant buildings as part of the Open House Programme. They could be anything from a grand 17th-century plantation house on a former sugar estate to a colonial-era seaside villa or historic church, and often they are beautifully decorated with antiques and sit in magnificent grounds. A garden party atmosphere prevails at these events, with fresh juices, rum punch, tea and snacks served on the lawns. Books on Barbados and the Caribbean are available for purchase, and artists and craftspeople sell their goods. Entry price is US$20, children (under 12) free. You can get the schedules and directions from the website and signs are erected to help visitors find the buildings. No booking is required; arrive at 1400 for a tour followed by a lecture at 1515 and tea at about 1545.

---

to keep anyone busy for a while, with several 18-hole and nine-hole courses, from the public Barbados Golf Club to the more exclusive Sandy Lane (where Tiger Woods got married). The **RBC Golf Classic** is held in November; the **Barbados Open** in September; the **Sir Garfield Sobers Festival of Golf Championships** in May and there are other competitions throughout the year. The **Barbados Golf Association** publishes a schedule of events, www.barbadosgolfassociation.com. See page 94 for details of the courses.

Hiking

The most beautiful part of the island is the Scotland District on the east coast. There is also some fine country along the St Lucy coast in the north and on the southeast coast. A particularly good hiking route is found along the old railway track from Bath to Bathsheba and on to Cattlewash. The Barbados Hiking Association, in association with the Barbados National Trust, organizes very enjoyable and sociable three-hour guided hikes every Sunday to various locations; see page 94.

Horse racing

Horse racing dates back to colonial times when planters challenged each other to races. Later the cavalry officers of the British Army joined in and by 1840 there were regular race days at the Garrison. Regular races are still held there, the biggest of which is the **Sandy Lane Barbados Gold Cup** held in March, which attracts racehorse owners from around the world. Again, this is something of a social occasion, with parties, parades and concerts. The Royal Barbados Mounted Police band leads a parade of dancers, tumblers and stiltmen in carnival fashion. See box, page 37.

Polo

An unusual spectator sport for a Caribbean island is polo, which appears to have been dropped in from the Home Counties and is followed avidly by mostly white expats. It has been played since cavalry officers introduced the game in the 19th century and the Polo Club was formed in 1884. Matches were originally played at the Garrison Savannah, where ponies were often reject racehorses, but there are now several polo fields on the island and its popularity has steadily risen. The season runs from just after Christmas until May, with lots of visiting teams from overseas coming to compete. See page 95.

Sailing

The main anchorage point for the sailing fraternity is Carlisle Bay, south of Bridgetown, home to the island's two yacht clubs: Barbados Yacht Club and the Barbados Cruising Club (page 35). In mid-January, the Round Barbados Sailing Week, www.roundbarbados.com, holds a series of races along the south and west coasts and the anti-clockwise Mount Gay Round Barbados Race. The first organized race around Barbados was held in 1936 when five trading schooners competed for 'bragging rights' and the winner took 10 hours and 20 minutes – today it takes roughly three to four hours for the quickest types of boat and if any records are broken the skipper wins his weight in Mount Gay rum. There are plenty of vantage points for spectators, and events at the Barbados Cruising Club.

There are lots of yachts and catamarans available for charter by the week, day or for shorter periods. Cruises up the west side of the island with stops for snorkelling and swimming with turtles are very popular, whether for lunch or sunset-watching. Larger catamarans can be cheaper but are often packed, so the smaller boats are likely to be more relaxed. See page 95.

Surfing

Because Barbados is exposed in the Atlantic, swells are driven towards the island from all directions, and surfing is good throughout the year with the larger waves occurring between October and March. The best and most consistent surfing is on the east coast at the Soup Bowl, which has perfect barrelling waves. Experienced surfers also like Duppies on the north coast, where you have a long paddle out and there is a lot of current, but the waves can be really big. The south coast is better for beginners and for boogie boarding, although there is a good break at Brandons, while the west coast has some good spots with easy access; try Sandy Lane, Tropicana, Gibbs and Maycock's.

There are regular national competitions and the main international event, the **Barbados Surf Pro**, is held at the Soup Bowl, Bathsheba, in March and is part of the World Surf League series. Barbados is a good place to learn and there are several surf schools. See page 96.

Windsurfing and kitesurfing

These are best along the south coast, where moderate winds are present all year and good 15-20 knot wind conditions from November to June. The centre of the action for windsurfers is Silver Rock where there's a 3 km stretch of reef providing excellent wave sailing on the outside and a sheltered lagoon and beach on the inside for beginners. Long Beach is the main kitesurfers' hang-out, with 2 km of undeveloped beachfront and cross-onshore northeast winds. Board rental and tuition is available. See page 97.

Where to stay

from ultra-luxurious hotels to B&Bs and everything in between

Tourism is the major industry on Barbados and there are literally hundreds of accommodation options, from all-inclusive luxury hotels and secluded beachfront villas to moderately priced family resorts and self-catering apartments. However, overall it is an upmarket destination and visitors come here for a treat, expecting – and receiving – excellent service and high standards. Accommodation rates tend to be higher than on some of the other less-popular Caribbean islands. Generally, the top hotels in the super-luxury category, costing well over US$1000 per person per night, are on the west or 'Platinum' coast. Places such as **Sandy Lane**, where you can get every conceivable service and luxury, are among the world's top resorts. Mid-range, cheerful places can be found all along the south coast for about US$190-380 per room, but many of these are characterless, concrete-block hotels usually booked as part of a package holiday; however, they offer a wide selection of amenities and are generally good value for families. There are far fewer places to stay on the east coast, where the landscape is rugged and breezy and air conditioning is rarely needed, but while many will enjoy the isolation and quiet, there is little choice of places to eat and no nightlife or shopping opportunities.

Although there are few budget options, there are apartment rentals and guesthouses, or you could opt for an apartment hotel where rooms have kitchenettes, and perhaps two double beds and/or pull-out sofa beds for children. It may mean giving up room service and direct access to the beach, and the décor

Price codes

Where to stay
$$$$ over US$380
$$$ US$190-380
$$ US$95-190
$ under US$95

Price codes refer to a standard double/twin room in high season.

Restaurants
$$$ over US$50
$$ US$25-50
$ under US$25

Price codes refer to the cost of a two-course meal, excluding drinks and service charge.

ON THE ROAD
Chattel houses

Dating from the colonial era, chattel houses are a distinctive part of Barbados' architectural and social heritage. These wooden houses all conformed to a basic, symmetrical plan, with a central door and a window either side, built on a foundation of loosely packed stones which allowed the air to circulate under and through the house. The steeply pitched roof would have originally been thatched but later they were all galvanized to withstand heavy winds and rain. Each chattel house was customized by its owners, who added pretty shutters, porches, jalousie windows, verandas and decorative detail such as gingerbread fretwork. The island's first chattel houses were built in the late 17th century, but they became more widespread after Emancipation in 1838. Although enslaved workers were freed, they were still landless and therefore had to rent small plots from the plantations on which they laboured. Laws provided the labourers the right to construct modest dwellings on these plots, but with the plantation owners having the right to evict tenants at will. As a result, the key feature of all chattel houses was that they could be dismantled and moved easily, so that if a worker moved from one plantation to another he could pack up and move with 'all his goods and chattels'.

may not be up to date or stylish, but there are some delightful, friendly options that start at around US$100-180 per night for two to four people. Costs can be brought down further by self-catering (supermarkets are well stocked with familiar brands from North America and some from the UK). Cleanliness and comfort are rarely an issue, and almost all rooms have air conditioning, TV and Wi-Fi.

High season, when rates are at their most expensive, is mid-December to mid-April. Out-of-season rates can drop significantly – up to 30-50% – so if a room or apartment sleeping four in a mid-range holiday resort costs around US$380-450 in the popular months, it could well be US$190-225 at other times; or as little as US$50 per person. Be aware, however, of the additional mandatory costs of a room charged across the board which when added up can make a holiday much more expensive than it first appears, and you will need to factor them into your budget. They are hotel VAT (10%) and service charge (10%); usually a single charge of 20%. Additionally, a room-rate levy (between US$4 and US$18 per night depending on the rate and accommodation class) must be paid locally and directly to the hotel. Be sure to check if these have or have not been included in final accommodation quotes. Rates are room only, B&B or all-inclusive; the latter meaning you get three meals a day and sometimes local drinks. Opting for an all-inclusive rate, or staying at a specifically all-inclusive resort (page 80) where everything such as watersports is included, can be appealing as you know exactly what you are getting for your money (especially if you combine flights and transfers in a package).

Food & drink

seafood, high-end gastronomy and, of course, rum punch

Just as Barbadian culture is a blend of British and African traditions, so the cuisine of Barbados is a mix of British and West African tastes and ingredients, developed over the centuries with some other flavours brought to the pot by immigrants from other nations, such as India. The need for carbohydrates to fuel slave labour and arduous work in the sugar cane fields has led to a diet based on starchy vegetables known as ground provisions, while difficulties in storing meat and fish in the tropical heat led to common use of salt meat and fish, pickles and other preserves. Sugar, the main crop of the island for generations, features heavily in both food and drink, reaching perfection in the production of rum.

Food

Fresh **fish** is excellent and sold at the markets in Oistins, Bridgetown and elsewhere in the late afternoon and evening, when the fishermen come in with their catch. It is a fascinating sight to watch the speed and skill with which women fillet flying fish and bag them up for sale. The main fish season is December-May, when there is less risk of stormy weather at sea. Flying fish is the national dish and a speciality with two or three fillets to a plate, eaten with chips, breaded in a sandwich (flying fish cutter) or with a sauce made from onions, tomatoes and herbs. Other popular and tasty fish include red snapper, wahoo or kingfish, barracuda, yellowfin tuna and 'dolphin fish' – the last being also called dorado or mahi mahi on restaurant menus, with no relation or resemblance to the mammal dolphin. There is also plenty of local crab, lobster, conch (*lambi*), octopus and shrimp/prawns.

Cou-cou is a filling starchy dish made from breadfruit or cornmeal with okra, peppers and hot sauce. *Jug-jug* is a Christmas speciality made from guinea corn, pigeon peas and salt meat, supposedly descended from the haggis of the poor white Scottish settlers exiled to the island after the failed Monmouth Rebellion of 1685. Pudding and souse is a huge dish of pickled breadfruit, black pudding and pork. Conkie is a corn-based dish often referred to as stew dumpling, traditionally made and sold during November, originally to celebrate the failure of Guy Fawkes' attempt to blow up the Houses of Parliament and King James I, and later to celebrate independence from British colonial rule. Conkie contains spices, sugar, pumpkin, cornmeal, coconut and sometimes raisins or cherries, all wrapped and steamed in a banana leaf, served hot.

There is a riot of tropical **fruit and vegetables**: unusual and often unidentifiable objects as well as more familiar items found in supermarkets in Europe and North America but with 10 times the flavour. The best bananas in the world are grown in the Caribbean; they are cheap, incredibly sweet and unlike anything you can buy at home. Many of the wonderful tropical fruits you will come across used in juices or in ice cream. Don't miss the rich flavours of the soursop, the guava or the sapodilla. Mangoes in season drip off the trees and those that don't end up on your breakfast plate can be found squashed in abundance all over the roads. Caribbean oranges are often green when ripe, as there is no cold season to bring out the orange colour, and are meant for juicing not peeling. Portugals are like tangerines and easy to peel. The grapefruit originated on Barbados in the 18th century, crossing a sweet orange and a bitter citrus called a shaddock, brought from Polynesia by Captain Shaddock. Avocados are nearly always sold unripe, so wait several days before attempting to eat them. Avocados have been around since the days of the Arawaks, who also cultivated cassava and cocoa, but many vegetables have their origins in the slave trade, brought over to provide a starchy diet for the slaves. The breadfruit, a common staple rich in carbohydrates and vitamins A, B and C, was brought from the South Seas in 1793 by Captain Bligh, perhaps more famous for the mutiny on the *Bounty*. It is eaten in a variety of ways on Barbados: with tomato and onion, a cucumber and lime souse, mashed like a potato or as wafer-thin crisps. It is one of the many forms of starch popular in local cooking; others include sweet potato, yam, eddo, green banana, plantain, bakes, cassava, rice, pasta and potato. Rice usually comes mixed with pigeon peas, black-eyed peas or split peas. Macaroni cheese is a popular accompaniment, and is referred to as 'pie'.

With sugar being grown on the island, Barbadians have developed a **sweet tooth**. It is worth trying tamarind balls, guava cheese, chocolate fudge and peanut brittle, while for dessert, coconut bread and Bajan baked custard and lemon meringue pie are firm favourites.

Drink

Barbados is a major producer of **rum** and you can find some excellent brands including Mount Gay, Cockspur, Malibu, Foursquare and St Nicholas Abbey. It is worth paying a bit extra for a good brand such as Old Gold, or for the slightly sweeter Sugar Cane Brandy, unless you are going to drink it with Coca-Cola, in which case anything will do. A rum and cream liqueur, *Crisma*, is popular in cocktails or on the rocks. Mount Gay produce a vanilla and a mango-flavoured rum. *Falernum* is sweet, sometimes slightly alcoholic, with a hint of vanilla and great in a rum cocktail instead of sugar syrup. If you drink in a rum shop, rum and other drinks are sold by the bottle. The smallest size is a mini, then a flask, then a full bottle. The shop will supply ice and glasses, you buy a mixer and serve yourself. 'Wine', in a rum shop, usually means sweet sherry and is often curiously mixed into a cocktail with ice and beer.

For **non-alcoholic drinks**, there is a range of refreshing fruit juices, including orange, mango, pineapple, grapefruit, lime, guava and passionfruit. *Sorrel* is a bright red drink made with hibiscus sepals and spices, and *mauby* is a bitter-sweet drink made from tree bark. Both are watered down like a fruit squash and they can be refreshing with lots of ice. Banks produces Bajan Light (a lager) as well as a milk stout and a non-alcoholic malt drink. Water is of excellent quality, as it comes mostly from deep wells sunk into the coral limestone, but there is bottled water if you prefer.

Tip...
Try coconut water – the clear liquid inside young green coconuts, which is very refreshing. A machete is often used to cut open the nut; look for barrows and stalls piled high with coconuts and a knife-wielding vendor in markets, on the side of village streets and in car parks at the beaches.

Eating out

It is not cheap to eat out on Barbados and even on a tight budget you could need up to US$65 per day for food and drink. Nevertheless, there are excellent restaurants, many of gourmet standard, especially along the west coast catering to the well-heeled visitors. Some of these are in the luxury hotels such as **Sandy Lane**, but you don't have to go to a hotel for cordon bleu cuisine. Many of the chefs are highly experienced, working in high-class kitchens in London or Paris before trying a spell in the Caribbean, bringing a variety of skills to the task of preparing tropical ingredients. Formal restaurants will charge around US$25-65 for a main course, but standards are high and the settings often special; you may get an open-air waterfront table or a garden terrace, perhaps even a table on the beach. The majority of places to eat are clustered around Holetown on the west coast and St Lawrence Gap on the south coast, where you can indulge in Italian, Mexican, Indian, French, Japanese or whatever takes your fancy. But there are ways of making your money go a little further. Eating where Bajans eat for lunch, for about US$10-15, includes cheap canteens in Bridgetown catering to office workers, take-away vans on the side of the road for the likes of flying fish cutters or filled rotis, or fast-food joints in shopping malls and along the south and west coasts (among others, Burger King, KFC and local brand

Chefette are present). It will cost two or three times that amount for lunch at a beach bar, especially for seafood and barbecue grills, but you can make a day of it with cocktails and sun loungers on the sand. Finally, you can grab takeaways from the supermarkets; Massy Stores branches have bakeries for bread and pastries as well as deli counters for salads, rotis and sandwiches, rotisserie chicken, cold meats and cheeses. Sadly, what is lacking are Bajan restaurants serving cheap, local food in the evenings, apart from a few rum shops selling fried chicken and the same fast-food places. However, on a Friday night, **Oistins Fish Fry** is a major event for both Barbadians and tourists; see box, page 74.

In terms of drinks, most cocktails using premium alcohol start at around US$13, but those made with rum will always be cheaper, while tasty local Banks beer at US$4-5 for a 500 ml bottle costs much less than imported brands. A bottle of wine in restaurants will range from about US$38 to upwards of US$500, soft drinks and water (330 ml) are US$3-5, and a cappuccino around US$4-5. The 17.5% VAT and a 2.5% product levy (20%) are included in menu prices but a service charge of 10% is added to the bill.

Bridgetown

The capital of Barbados, Bridgetown sits on Carlisle Bay on the southwest corner of the island and has a population of around 110,000. The centre is small and compact but always busy and full of life. Swan Street is a lively pedestrian street where Barbadians do their shopping and street musicians sometimes perform; on Broad Street you will find a whole range of sophisticated shops catering for tourists, with malls, duty-free shops and department stores. On the northern side of the Careenage is National Heroes Square, which celebrates the 10 figures that shaped the modern history of Barbados, and the pleasant wooden Bridgetown Boardwalk, where old converted warehouses and restaurants overlook boats plying their trade on the inlet. Another interesting place to visit is the Garrison Historic Area; inscribed as a UNESCO World Heritage Site in 2011, it has a horse-racing track and a number of fine old buildings dating back to the British colonial times. The suburbs of Bridgetown sprawl along the south and west coasts and quite a long way inland; many areas are very pleasant, full of flowering trees and 19th-century coral stone gingerbread villas.

Central Bridgetown
the island's business centre, with shops, restaurants, waterside squares and a boardwalk

Broad Street and around

Previously called Exchange Street and New England Street, Broad Street is Bridgetown's main road and business area and is lined with shops, small malls, banks, offices and fast-food restaurants. It runs east to west from Fairchild Street to Cheapside Road, and colonial-style buildings dating back to the 1800s rub shoulders with more modern buildings. Many of the shops are devoted to cruise-ship passengers and sell souvenirs and duty-free jewellery, cameras, cosmetics, perfumes, alcoholic beverages and the like. The most notable is **Bridgetown Duty Free** ⓘ *10-14 Broad St, T539 4400, www.bridgetowndutyfree.com, Mon-Sat 0830-1730*, near the top end of Broad Street close to National Heroes Square. This large duty-free department store and mall was once a Cave Shepherd store, originally established by Bridgetown businessmen, Mr R G Cave and Mr J P Shepherd, as a dry goods store in 1907. Right next door is another upmarket mall, the **Norman Centre**, where on the first floor is the **Caribbean Wax Museum** ⓘ *corner of Broad and Middle streets, T268 1760, Tue-Sat 1000-1630, US$10, children (under 12) US$5*. This unexpected find was created by Barbadian artists Arthur Edwards and Frances Ross and displays life-sized popular Caribbean characters. They're not actually made in wax: the pair used store mannequins and silicone rubber and resin to replicate skin and the results are surprisingly good – children will love it. The 30 or so figures include politicians like Barbados' first Prime Minister Errol Walton, and personalities in popular culture and sports including Jamaican sprinter Usain Bolt, cricketers Brian Lara and Sir Garfield Sobers, musician Bob Marley and, naturally, Barbados-born Rihanna holding her first Grammy award. At the lower end of Lower Broad Street, on the corner of Prince Alfred Street, look out for the beautiful **Mutual Building**, which was built in 1895 as the Barbados Mutual Life Assurance Society Building and is presently a branch of First Citizens Bank. It is a

Essential Bridgetown

Finding your feet

The Adams Barrow Cummins (ABC) Highway runs from the Grantley Adams International Airport in Christ Church in the east, to Cave Hill Road and the University of the West Indies in Saint Michael on the west coast, and roughly skirts the metropolitan area of Bridgetown. Several roundabouts along the highway give access into Bridgetown. There is also a road along the south coast, Highway 7, which runs from Oistins in the east through the main resort area on the south coast, and enters the city through the Garrison Historical Area. Highway 1 runs down the west coast and comes into the capital as the Mighty Grynner (Spring Garden) Highway. Buses and route taxis run frequently on all these routes in and out of Bridgetown; out-of-town bus stops are marked simply 'To City' or 'Out of City'.

Getting around

The centre of Bridgetown is easily toured on foot, while buses, route taxis and taxis are available for venturing further afield.

Tip...

On the JTC Ramsay roundabout at the junction of the ABC Highway and Highway 5, keep an eye out for the striking, bronze, 2.75 m-high Bussa Emancipation Statue, which is of slave rebellion leader Bussa 'breaking from chains'.

very tall, grey Victorian structure topped with twin silver domes and a fine overhanging iron veranda on the second floor. In 2011 it became a designated property within the UNESCO World Heritage Site of Historic Bridgetown and its Garrison.

West towards Deep Water Harbour and opposite the General Post Office, **Cheapside Public Market** ⓘ *Cheapside, T426 4463, Mon-Thu 0700-1800, Fri-Sat 0700-2000*, is an excellent and colourful fresh fruit and vegetable market in both a double-storey indoor part and an outdoor section of stalls. There's a great assortment of Caribbean produce for sale, like sweet potatoes, yams, eddos, breadfruits, green bananas and cassavas, and some stalls sell souvenirs. Upstairs there are food stalls; look out for saltfish bake, fried plantain and breadfruit, and ginger and cucumber iced drinks.

A short 300 m walk southwest and on Princess Alice Highway, opposite Princess Alice Bus Terminal, is the modern and organized **Bridgetown Fish Market** ⓘ *T431 0202, daily 0730-1600*. Many of the islands' restaurants buy their 'catch of the day' here and there's a great choice including flying fish, kingfish, mahi mahi, billfish, tuna and swordfish; the ladies will fillet it and pack with ice.

Across the road and next to the bus terminal, the **Pelican Craft Centre** ⓘ *Mon-Sat 0800-2200, Sun 0900-1500* (page 92) is a great place to buy souvenirs in shops inside

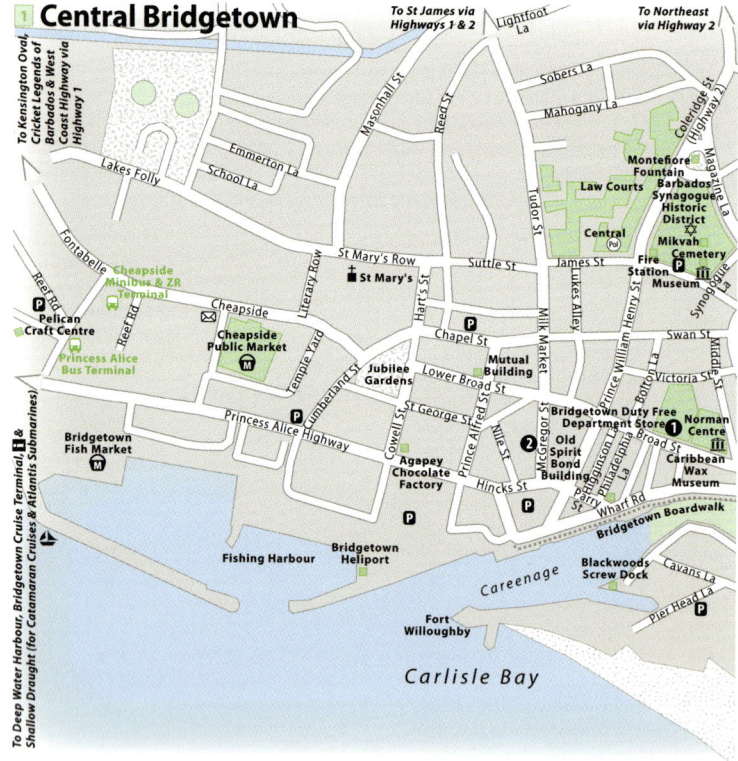

28 • **Barbados** Bridgetown

replica chattel houses, and it's very popular with cruise passengers given it's only a 900 m walk from Bridgetown Cruise Terminal further west. It's named after brown pelicans that nested on Pelican Island until 1961, when it was merged with the mainland to accommodate the extension of the Deep Water Harbour. Over Christmas and during busier tourist seasons, **Bridgetown Night Market** is held here on Fridays: shops stay open later and there's additional craft, cocktail and food stalls.

Cricket Legends of Barbados

ⓘ Herbert House, Fontabelle Rd, T537 2651, see Facebook. Mon-Fri 0900-1600, US$13, under 12s half price, 30 min tours until 1530.

About 850 m northwest up Fontabelle Road from Cheapside Public Market, and (naturally) directly opposite the Kensington Oval, this small but comprehensive museum is a must for those who enjoyed watching West Indies test cricket from the late 1950s to the 1990s. It's full of memorabilia from cricket bats and balls to shirts personally donated by players, as well as old radio commentary, photos and interesting newspaper articles, and the guides talk through the intricacies of the game. It was established by Windies cricket legend Desmond Haynes (who lucky visitors might well meet as he's often there) and pays tribute to all the great

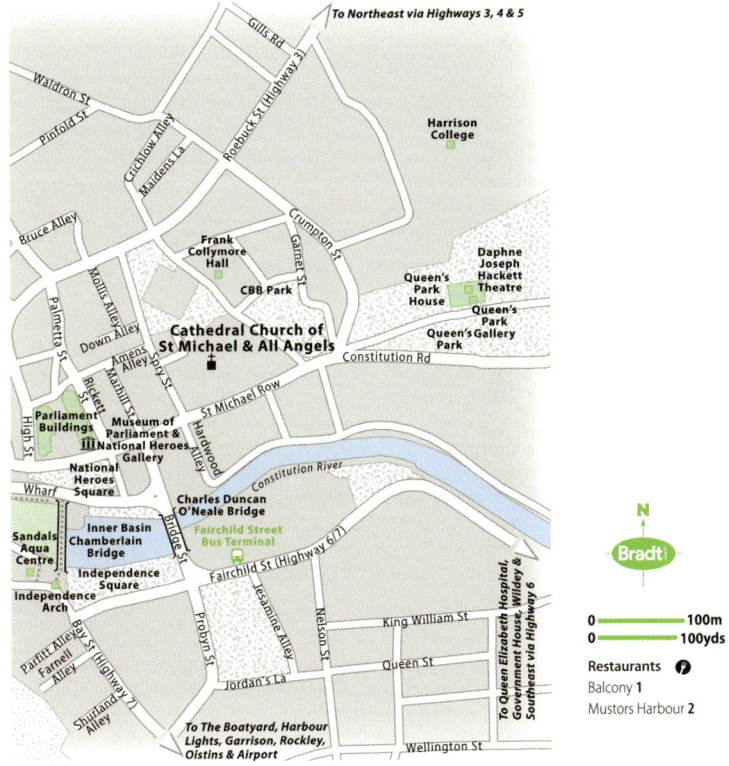

BACKGROUND
Bridgetown

Bridgetown was once known as Indian Bridge, named after a basic wooden bridge across the Careenage. It is believed that the bridge was left behind by the Arawak Indians or Caribs who had inhabited the island before the 1500s. The British removed the structure and built a new bridge sometime after 1654 and the area became known as the Town of Saint Michael and, later, Bridgetown. The Careenage is an inlet of water at the mouth of Constitution River, where schooners and trading vessels transporting sugar, rum and molasses to the larger ships in Carlisle Bay used to tie up. It got its name because the boats were careened on to their sides so that the hulls could be cleaned or mended. In 1657, a portion of the waterfront was declared a public wharf; between 1837 and 1846 a new extended wharf was constructed under the direction of the Royal Engineers stationed with the British Garrison; in 1887 a dry dock was completed on the southern side; and to this, a screw lifting dock was added in 1893 so ships could be lifted completely out of the water for better repairs (the remains of Blackwoods Screw Dock, named after its creator John Blackwood, can be seen off Cavans Lane where there are museum signboards explaining how it worked). By the end of the 1800s, Bridgetown was a major centre for ship maintenance and repair in the Caribbean; the island was often the first landfall for ships coming from Europe. Nowadays, cargo and cruise ships dock at the Deep Water Harbour to the north, which is still one of the most advanced ports in the Caribbean; it has been dredged so it can accommodate the largest cruise ships in the world. However, the Careenage is still used for recreational and tourist-based small craft such as catamarans and sport fishing boats that tout their wares to visitors. Two bridges now separate the outer and inner basins of the Careenage – Chamberlain Bridge and Charles Duncan O'Neal Bridge – and in 1999, the Wickham Lewis Boardwalk was built along Wharf Road on the northern side.

Barbados players such as Sir Wesley Hall, Malcolm Marshall, Clyde Walcott, Everton Weekes and Frank Worrell. A whole room is dedicated to legendary Sir Garfield Sobers, considered by many to be cricket's greatest ever all-rounder, and one of the 10 National Heroes of Barbados.

Across the road, cricket fans can continue their pilgrimage by taking a tour of the pitch at the **Kensington Oval** ⓘ *tours begin at the security booth on President Kennedy Drive, T536 0351, www.kensingtonoval.org, Mon-Fri, four times daily, from US$10, children (under 12) US$5*. Bridgetown's historic Oval was established in 1882 when Pickwick Cricket Club leased 1.6 ha (4 acres) of pasture from Kensington Plantation, and it first hosted a Test Match in 1930 when the West Indies and England played to a draw. Its most significant upgrade during its long history was for the 2007 Cricket World Cup and it now seats 11,000. Near the entrance is a bronze statue of Sir Garfield Sobers.

National Heroes Square

This small, triangular 'square', between Broad Street and the north side of the Careenage, is the hub of central Bridgetown. It used to be called Trafalgar Square and there is a statue there of Lord Nelson, sculpted by Sir Richard Westmacott and predating its London equivalent by 30 years. Admiral Nelson visited Barbados with his fleet in 1805, a few months before his death, and the square was named the following year; the statue was erected on 22 March

1813 to commemorate the anniversary of the British Royal Navy's victory in the Battle of Trafalgar in 1805. Over the years the name became the subject of some controversy as it was thought to link Barbados too closely with its colonial past. As a result, Nelson was turned through 180° so that he no longer looked down Broad Street, and in 1999 Trafalgar Square was renamed National Heroes Square after the 10 people who shaped the modern history of Barbados; they are also remembered on National Heroes Day, which was first celebrated on 28 April 1998, the centenary of the birth of Sir Grantley Adams. Other features of the square are the Cenotaph War Memorial, with its grey granite obelisk built in 1925 to commemorate Barbadians who died during the First World War, and the Dolphin Fountain, constructed in 1865 to commemorate the piping of water to Bridgetown in 1861.

Parliament Buildings

Across Broad Street to the north of the square are the neo-Gothic Parliament Buildings with their red roofs and green shutters. Founded in 1639, Barbados has the third-oldest parliament in the Commonwealth, after Britain and Bermuda. The present buildings, where both the lower house (House of Assembly) and the upper house (Senate) still meet weekly, were completed in 1873. The east wing, housing the House of Assembly and Senate, has stained-glass windows depicting British kings and queens from James I to Queen Victoria, as well as the Lord Protector Oliver Cromwell. The **clock tower** on the west wing dates from 1886 and was originally located on the east wing, but within 10 years of its construction it began to sink and crack and had to be demolished in 1884; the redesigned clock tower and reassembled clock were moved to the west wing in 1880. Today the west wing houses public offices as well as the **Museum of Parliament and National Heroes Gallery** ⓘ *T310 5400, www.barbadosparliament.com, Mon, Wed-Fri 1000-1600, Sat 1000-1500, US$10, children (under 3) free, closed for maintenance at the time of writing*. This is a simple but well-staffed and interesting museum which brings snippets of Barbados' history alive with murals, artefacts, quotes, videos and photographs. It's also refreshingly air-conditioned, so makes a fine cooling break on a hot walk around the centre of Bridgetown. The National Heroes Gallery is particularly interesting, documenting the achievements of the nine men and one woman who contributed to Barbadian history. Admission includes a guided tour of both houses of Parliament (if the Senate or the House of Assembly are sitting on the day, you can re-use your ticket on another day).

Chamberlain Bridge and around

Running south from the square is Chamberlain Bridge, for centuries one of the capital's two main bridges and built roughly in the same place as the old Indian Bridge. It was originally a swing bridge constructed between 1861 and 1872 and was named at the beginning of the 20th century in honour of Joseph Chamberlain, British Secretary of State for the Colonies, who gave the island a large chunk of money in grants and loans to keep the economy afloat. It was rebuilt in 2006 as a pedestrian and lift bridge – to allow entry for boats into the inner basin of the Careenage – adjoining the refurbished coral stone arch structure dating from 1861. There is a plaque with the Barbados national anthem on the bridge, while **Independence Arch**, at the southern end of the bridge, was built in 1987 to celebrate 21 years of independence; look out for some of the national symbols painted on the pillars, including a flying fish, a pelican and the Pride of Barbados flower.

To the east of the arch and bridge and running between the southern side of the Careenage and Fairchild Street to Charles Duncan O'Neal Bridge (page 32), **Independence Square** is a recreational square and garden with a view across the inner basin of the Careenage to National Heroes Square and the Parliament Buildings. It was refurbished in 2007 and has seating areas, an amphitheatre for public events and concerts (Diana Ross and the Supremes performed here in celebration to Barbados on its second night of self-government in 1966), two fountains and a bronze statue of Errol Walton Barrow, the first Prime Minister of Barbados (1966-1976) who had a political career that lasted 36 years up until his death in 1987; he is one of the 10 National Heroes of Barbados.

To the west of Chamberlain Bridge, along Wharf Street on the northern side of the Careenage, is the wooden **Bridgetown Boardwalk**. Its official name is **Wickham Lewis Boardwalk**, after Clennell Wickham (1896-1938), a radical journalist and newspaper editor, and T T Lewis (1905-1959), a politician. Featuring vintage-style street lamps and benches and a number of shops and cafés, it offers a good view of the yachts, charter fishing boats and catamarans docked in the Careenage. About halfway along, on the corner of Parry Street, the red-brick **Old Spirit Bond Building** dates back to the 18th century when it was a warehouse for rum and other spirits. From here, barrels were loaded on to small boats in the Careenage and then transported to cargo ships docked offshore in Carlisle Bay. The building has been restored and is now home to small businesses. At the western end of the boardwalk is a small park which celebrates Barbados' maritime heritage, complete with cannons (originally from James Fort) and plaques with interesting facts about Barbados pirates. About 500 m west of Chamberlain Bridge, the **Agapey Chocolate Factory** ⓘ *Hincks St, T424 2739, www.agapey.com, Mon-Fri 0930-1600, Sat 1000-1500*, sells delicious homemade artisan dark chocolate (and ice cream) using local cane sugar and rum to flavour cocoa from Ecuador, Grenada and the Dominican Republic. One-hour 'bean to bar' factory tours are conducted with prior reservation.

Charles Duncan O'Neal Bridge

The second bridge over the Careenage, going off southeast from National Heroes Square, is named after another of the National Heroes of Barbados, Charles Duncan O'Neal (1879-1936), a physician by trade who worked on behalf of the poor and the disadvantaged and established the Democratic League in 1924 and the Working Men's Association in 1926; in 1932 he was elected to the House of Assembly. The first bridge here was completed in 1681 and was funded by levying a tax on slaves. It was pulled down in 1967 and replaced with a wider, stronger, more modern structure designed to take the increased volume of traffic. If you are driving, the junctions can be a bit scary until you get the hang of the one-way system as locals drive very fast over the river and away; the Fairchild Street Bus Terminal creates an extra hazard on the south side of the bridge.

Cathedral Church of Saint Michael and All Angels

St Michael Row, T427 0790, www.saintmichaelscathedral.bb. Tue-Sat 0900-1700, Sun 0700-1200, Sun services various times from 0700 to 1800 (see website), free but donations appreciated.

Take the northeast exit out of National Heroes Square along St Michael Row to reach this 18th-century Anglican cathedral with its fine set of inscriptions and a single-hand clock. The first building was consecrated in 1665 but was destroyed by a hurricane in 1780. The present cathedral is long and broad with a balcony, a huge barrel-vaulted ceiling, galleries on three sides, stained-glass windows and some tombs (1675) built into the porch. Completed in 1789 with £10,000 raised in a lottery, it became a cathedral in 1825 with the arrival of Bishop Coleridge, but suffered hurricane damage in 1831. Sir Grantley Adams and his son, Tom Adams, both prime ministers, are buried here along with other famous Barbadians.

Queen's Park and around

If you continue east on St Michael Row you reach Queen's Park, a pleasant, restful park just outside the city centre, which shares parts of its grounds with Harrison College and the headquarters of the Barbados Transport Board. It's home to the largest tree on Barbados: a 28 m-tall baobab with a circumference of 18 m, thought to be over 1000 years old. Baobabs originated in Guinea and the tree is believed to have floated across the Atlantic and rooted itself on the edge of a lagoon. The park and its fountain were designed by Lady Gilbert Carter, the wife of the governor, who opened the gates in 1909 with a golden key. **Queen's Park House**, a beautiful building dating from 1786, was once the residence of the general commanding the British troops in the West Indies (it was known as King's House until Queen Victoria came to the throne), and in the 20th century it became a small theatre and art gallery. After being closed for a number of years, the lovely house was completely restored and reopened in 2017, and it is now one of the listed buildings within the UNESCO World Heritage Site of Historic Bridgetown and its Garrison. Once again it's home to the **Daphne Joseph Hackett Theatre** (page 91), and the **Queen's Park Gallery** (page 91), both run by the National Cultural Foundation (*www.ncf.bb*).

Further east still is **Government House**, first known as Pilgrim House. Purchased for the Government in 1736 from John Pilgrim, a Quaker, it is a typical example of a plantation great house, with arched porticoes, jalousie window shutters, verandas, a parapet roof and a circular driveway, as well as delightful gardens. The home and office of the governor-general of Barbados, it is sometimes included in the Barbados National Trust's Open House Programme (see box, page 18).

Swan Street

Back in the centre and parallel to Broad Street, busy Swan Street is the second most popular shopping area in Bridgetown. It was named after John Swann, the surveyor who laid out the principal streets in 1656. In the early years it was also known as Jew Street because it was mainly populated by Jewish merchants, who had shops and businesses on the ground level and lived upstairs; by the late 17th century, Jews had almost exclusive control over imported goods from Europe. After a destructive fire in 1845, this street, along with many properties in the lower Bridgetown area, became known as the 'Burnt District'. Today Swan Street is a pedestrian paved street lined with shops and stalls (generally cheaper than on Broad Street).

Nidhe Israel Synagogue and Museum

Synagogue Lane, parking from James St, T436 6869, www.synagoguehistoricdistrict.com. Synagogue & Museum, Mon-Fri 0900-1500, Historic Fire Brigade Station & Café, Mon-Fri 1130-1500, Sat-Sun 0930-1500, US$12.50.

A block north of Swan Street, this beautifully restored place of worship is an early 19th-century building on the site of a 17th-century one, one of the two earliest synagogues in the western hemisphere. The original one was built in 1654 by Jews fleeing Recife, Brazil, who heard that Oliver Cromwell had granted freedom of worship for Jews. Cromwell granted the first pass to settle in 1655 to Dr Abraham de Mercado, an elder of the Recife society, and his son David Rafael. By the 1680s there were 300 Jews on Barbados, or 5% of the total population, and by the middle of the 18th century there were 800. They were heavily involved in the sugar industry, advancing capital and credit or owning plantations. The synagogue was destroyed by a hurricane in 1831, and the present building was constructed on the old foundations and reopened in 1833. However, by 1929 the Jewish community on the island had all but migrated and the synagogue fell into disrepair.

A small revival of Jewish residents on the island began with a few Polish Jews fleeing

Europe in the late 1930s en route to Venezuela. They started working as peddlers, gradually attracted friends and other family members, and the community grew again. Painstakingly restored by this community, with the support of the Barbados National Trust, the Caribbean Conservation Association and the Barbados government, the synagogue reopened in 2008. In 2017 the community designated the **Barbados Synagogue Historic District**, which covers the whole block bounded by James Street, Coleridge Street, Magazine Lane and Synagogue Lane. It includes beautiful grounds, the Jewish cemetery, and other buildings such as Bridgetown's first fire station (1858), which is now a café, and the former rabbi's house next to the synagogue that is a museum exhibiting a timeline of Jewish settlement on Barbados. The most significant component is a full immersion mikvah (ritual bath) unearthed by archaeologists in 2008 and believed to have been built with the original synagogue in 1654; it's the only one known to exist in the Americas.

In a small garden at the junction of Coleridge Street and Magazine Lane, at the north end of the Barbados Synagogue Historic District, is the **Montefiore Fountain**. It was built as a drinking water fountain in 1864 by Jewish businessman John Montefiore in memory of his father, a leading merchant who died of cholera. It was originally in Beckwith Place on Lower Broad Street, but was moved to Coleridge Street in 1940 and there is no water connected to it. The statues on each face of the fountain represent Justice, Fortitude, Temperance and Prudence.

Bay Street

Bay Street runs south of the city centre from the two bridges and Independence Square, hugging the edge of **Carlisle Bay**, which was named after the Earl of Carlisle, James Hay, who was Lord Proprietor of Barbados in the 1600s. Bay Street is part of Highway 7, the main route between Bridgetown and the south coast. Along this part of the bay is **Brownes Beach**, which has broad white sands, calm, clear water with small waves and almost no undertow. It is a surprisingly good beach considering how close it is to town. Yachts anchor here, snorkelling and diving parties call in and there are beach facilities such as sun loungers and umbrellas, and lifeguards are on duty. With beach bars and restaurants and a number of watersports operators, it's a lively area with lots of action, and is often packed with cruise-ship visitors.

At the northern end of Brownes Beach, and only 600 m south of Chamberlain Bridge, **The Boatyard** ⓘ *Bay St, T826 4448, www.theboatyard.com, daily 0900-1800, day pass US$35, children (4-12) US$20*, is a beach club with non-stop music, restaurant, bar, changing facilities, showers and watersports kiosk. The day pass includes loungers/umbrellas, ocean trampoline, dive platform, rope swing and a short snorkelling trip by boat. Another 500 m south, **Harbour Lights** ⓘ *Bay St, T436 7225, www.harbourlightsbarbados.com, daily 0900-1700*, has similar facilities with a minimum spend of US$10 for a lounger/umbrella, plus there are turtle/shipwreck snorkelling tours (from US$35), jet skis (US$60), and a good restaurant/bar with service to the beach. It becomes a popular dinner/show venue and nightclub in the evening (page 89).

At the southern end of Brownes Beach, opposite the Prime Minister's Office and other government offices, is the **Bay Street Esplanade** – a small park and promenade featuring a bandstand dating from 1919 and a statue of Sir Grantley Adams. It has benches and lawns popular for barbecues and sunset-watching. A little further south, and contrary to the name, **Pebbles Beach** is another swathe of pure white sand. On most mornings from about 0600, grooms walk racehorses down from the Garrison for an hour's exercise on the beach, and often the horses can be seen frolicking in the calm surf and even swimming. Pebbles Beach is also the location of the island's two sailing clubs. The **Barbados Yacht Club** ⓘ *Bay St, T427 1125, www.barbadosyachtclub.com*, is a private members' club (visiting yachts are given a seven-day membership) which holds colourful regattas in Carlisle Bay at weekends. The largest is the **Old Brigand Rum Regatta**, usually in the middle of March. The **Barbados Cruising Club** ⓘ *Aquatic Gap, T425 5434, www.barbadoscruisingclub.org*, is again a private members' club, but non-members are welcome to eat and drink at **Skipper's Beach Bar** ⓘ *daily 1200-2200, happy hour 1700-1900*. The club hosts Barbados' biggest sailing event, the **Round Barbados Sailing Week** (*www.roundbarbados.com*; page 19), which attracts hundreds of racing boats from all over the Caribbean in the middle of January. This is a wonderful event to watch from Bay Street and the races can also be seen from various points around the island. For more information on sailing, see page 95.

The offshore **Carlisle Bay Marine Park** is a favourite spot for diving and snorkelling excursions, with a series of interlocking marine trails roughly marked out underwater by old cannons, anchors and pylons leading the way from one wreck to the next. There are five shallow wrecks in the bay: the *Berwyn*, the *Fox*, the *C-Trec*, the *Bajan Queen* and the *Eillon*. The *Bajan Queen*, a tugboat converted to a party boat before being sunk in 2002, sits only a few metres underwater so is perfect for snorkelling or diving, and is growing a variety of coral as well as being home to plenty of fish. The *Berwyn* was a French First World War tugboat sunk in 1919 by her own crew; because of her age, this wreck is covered in healthy hard and soft coral growth and associated reef creatures.

★Garrison Historic Area

an excellent example of 18th-century British military architecture

South of central Bridgetown is the Garrison area on the strategic southeast point of the island guarding the entrance to Carlisle Bay and the capital. During the 18th century the Caribbean was the scene of numerous military conflicts, primarily between Britain and France who fought for supremacy. In the face of a possible French invasion in 1785, a permanent garrison was built and Barbados became the headquarters of the Windward and Leeward command of the British forces in the region. It was the largest of its kind in the British Colonies, and included hospitals, barracks and houses in the Georgian and Palladian style with grand staircases, arcades and pediments. However, by the late 19th century the British decided to reduce their forces in the region, and by 1905 most of the last regiments had left the island. In 2011, Historic Bridgetown and its Garrison became a UNESCO World Heritage Site as 'an outstanding example of British colonial architecture', and today there are a number of historically significant buildings to visit.

Garrison Savannah

The 61 ha (151 acre) Garrison Historic Area covers an area from the Bay Street Esplanade to Hastings on the south coast. The focal point is the 13 ha (30 acre) Garrison Savannah (or just the 'Savannah'), once a swamp before it was drained by the Royal Engineers in the early 1800s to become a parade ground for soldiers and the place where they trained and drilled. It was surrounded by a six-furlong racecourse in 1845, first used by regimental officers whose horses competed against those of wealthy plantation owners. Still a popular racecourse, it is now the home of the **Barbados Turf Club** (see box, opposite), and is used at other times for exercising the horses, early morning or evening jogging, and informal rugby and basketball games; there's usually something going on on Sunday afternoons. Along Garrison Road and the roads leading off are numerous 17th- to 19th-century military buildings constructed on traditional British colonial lines from brick brought as ballast on ships from England. Painted in bright colours, some now contain government offices, while others are places of business or private homes.

> **Tip...**
> Every Thursday, the Barbados Legion, the retirement arm of the Barbados Defence Force, pays tribute to the military history of Barbados by re-enacting the Changing of the Sentry ceremony at the Main Guard. Up to 13 men in full ceremonial dress – the Zouave uniform selected by Queen Victoria in 1858 for the West India Regiment – march past the sentry post at the clock tower. This presentation starts at 1145 and lasts approximately 15 minutes until the clock chimes at noon. The sentries take their annual holiday in September.

There are several memorials around the oval racecourse. In the southwest corner is one commemorating the 'awful' hurricane which killed 14 men and one woman and caused the destruction of the barracks and hospital on 18 August 1831; outside the Barbados Museum in the northeast corner there's another to the men of the Royal York Rangers who fell in action against the French in Martinique, Les Saintes and Guadeloupe in the 1809-1810 campaign.

Main Guard

On Garrison Road, the Main Guard overlooks the racecourse from the western side. Built in 1804, it is one of the most outstanding buildings in the Garrison Historic Area. It is of elegant Georgian style and the main house, with its Roman arched portico and pediment, has a George III coat of arms designed especially for the building, a handsome clock tower, a fine wide veranda (or gallery in Caribbean terms) with cast-iron trimmings, and there's a guardhouse at the rear. It was used as the main guard command and central military police station during the 1800s until 1905, when the British forces withdrew. Today the property is home to several organizations, including the Barbados Legion and Barbados Poppy League. Outside is an impressive array of 26 cannons (part of the National Cannon Collection, page 39) mounted on metal garrison gun carriages (replaced with wooden ones during action as they were prone to shatter).

Barbados Museum

Dalkeith Rd, T538 0201, see Facebook. Mon-Sat 0900-1700, US$10, children (under 12) US$5.

On the northeast corner of the Savannah, this museum is housed in the former British Military Prison; its upper section was built in 1817 and lower section in 1853. It became the Barbados Museum and headquarters of the Historical Society from 1930. It is well set out through a series of 10 galleries, and exhibits include a fine map gallery with the earliest map of Barbados by Richard Ligon (1657), colonial-era furniture, military history (including a reconstruction of a prisoner's cell), prints and paintings which depict social life in the West Indies, decorative and domestic arts (17th- to 19th-century glass, china and silver), and a gallery about slavery and African people in the Caribbean. The staff are

ON THE ROAD
Horsing around

Horse racing is surprisingly popular on the Caribbean islands that have sufficient flat land to build a racetrack and even on some where there isn't. Like many sports it is seen as an opportunity for a party and the crowd is enthusiastic, even if not particularly knowledgeable, although never underestimate Bajans when it comes to betting. In Bridgetown there has been horse racing on the Garrison Savannah since 1845 and the **Barbados Turf Club** *(T626 3980, www.barbadosturfclub.org, ticket office at the Grandstand, Mon-Sat 0800-1600)* was established in 1905. The track is a 6-furlong oval grass strip with the horses running in a clockwise direction. The Grandstand gives you a good vantage point because it is elevated, but anywhere around the track is good to watch the racing, and you can get right up close to the action by the parade ring, the finish line or when the jockeys make their way to the weighing room. The betting booths and food and drink stalls are never far away, and there is entertainment from 1300 to 1800.

    The most prestigious event of the year is the Sandy Lane Barbados Gold Cup, a thoroughbred race run annually in late February/early March since 1982 and sponsored by Sandy Lane since 1997. The Gold Cup attracts racehorse owners from around the world. There are crowds, stalls, noise, merriment and lots of entertainment, from dancers to regimental bands. Nine races are held on the day with the most important being the penultimate one that is run over a distance of 1800 m (8.95 furlongs). All the excitement builds up to see who will win the gold trophy, usually presented to the winner by the Prime Minister of Barbados. At other times of the year, race meetings are held on Saturday afternoons during three seasons: January-April, May-August and November-December. Entry to the Grandstand is from US$13 (no children under 12), and to the Field Stand and Sir John Chandler Stand, the flatter areas on either side of the Grandstand and around the track, US$8. Higher entry fees apply for the Sandy Lane Barbados Gold Cup and Boxing Day races, and on bank holidays.

very knowledgeable about the history of the island and the museum shop has a good selection of craft items, books, prints and cards.

George Washington House and Garrison Tunnels
Bush Hill, off Garrison Rd, T228 5461, daily 0900-1600, US$20, children (5-12) US$10, under 5s free; self-guided visit to the house, museum, and areas of the tunnels (but guided tours can be arranged with advance notice for US$100).

North of the Main Guard at the northwest corner of the Savannah, this beautifully restored 18th-century plantation house is where the future first president of the USA stayed in 1751 for a few months when, as a 19-year-old, he accompanied his sick brother Lawrence (who later died) to search for a cure for his TB. This was George Washington's only excursion outside his homeland and Bridgetown was the largest town he had seen. At that time, health care was more advanced on Barbados than it was in the United States. While in Bridgetown, Washington was introduced to the delights of the theatre and banquets where he met the leading scientists, engineers and military strategists of the day. He contracted smallpox but the skill of a British doctor saved him. As a result, he acquired

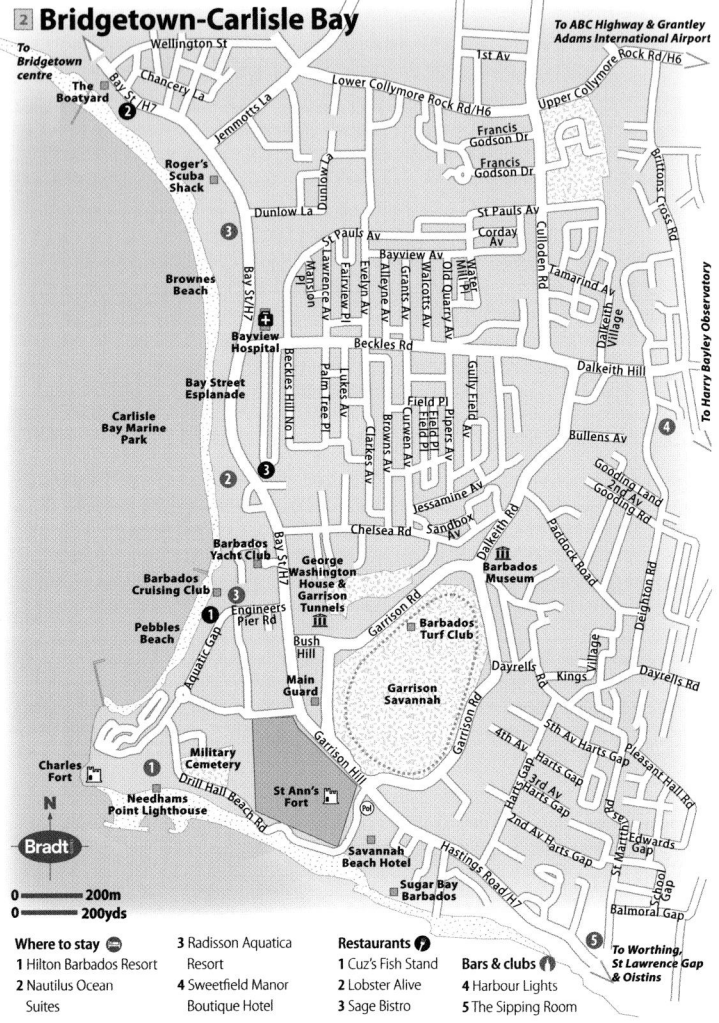

Bridgetown-Carlisle Bay

Where to stay
1 Hilton Barbados Resort
2 Nautilus Ocean Suites
3 Radisson Aquatica Resort
4 Sweetfield Manor Boutique Hotel

Restaurants
1 Cuz's Fish Stand
2 Lobster Alive
3 Sage Bistro

Bars & clubs
4 Harbour Lights
5 The Sipping Room

immunity to the virus which enabled him to survive an outbreak of the disease during the American War of Independence, which killed many of his men.

The house went on to become Bush Hill House, a residence for officers within the Garrison, including the Commander of the Royal Engineers. After the withdrawal of the British in 1905, it returned to private ownership until it was restored and opened to the public in 2007. The ground floor is furnished as it might have been in 1751 when Washington stayed, while the second floor displays items typical of life in the mid-18th century, from medical appliances to agricultural implements; there's a section on the plantation economy and slavery and how it related to Washington, a slave owner himself.

Access to the Garrison Tunnels is from George Washington House. The tunnel below the house was rediscovered quite by accident in 2011 during preparation work for the relocation of the café. After exploration, this tunnel was found to extend far beyond the boundaries of the property and joins a 3 km network of at least nine other tunnels under the Savannah area, with others extending into the west of the Garrison's 61 ha (151 acres). The restored section under George Washington House that is open to the public is about 60 m in length, 60 cm wide and 2.5-3.5 m high. It is believed that these mysterious arched-roof tunnels carved through limestone rock date from about 1820 and were used as a drainage course for the then swampy Savannah, and also to facilitate the secret movement of soldiers.

> **Tip...**
> Coffee Barbados Café, in the old 1830s stable building of George Washington House (*T833 8051, see Facebook, Mon-Fri 0730-1600, Sat 0900-1600*) serves breakfast, lunch and cakes/pastries, and has a wonderful view of the gardens (you can visit without paying house entry fees).

St Ann's Fort

South of the Main Guard on the southwest side of the Savannah, St Ann's Fort was built in 1705 and, during the 1800s, a lookout was added and it became the main command post and communication point for the six signal stations located around the island. The long, thin Drill Hall was built on to the walls of the fort in 1790 as barracks for the soldiers, and in 1881 the building became the headquarters for the Garrison until the British left in 1905. In 1979, it became the Officers' Mess and Sergeants' Mess of the Barbados Defence Force, and the fort remains their headquarters today. You cannot enter but look for the crenellated signal tower with its flagpole on top.

The **Barbados National Armoury** ⓘ *access via the Barbados Defence Force reception, T536 2500, www.bdfbarbados.com; 1½ hr tours by appointment only with the Barbados Defence Force, US$25 for 1-5 people, US$5 per additional person up to 12; alternatively a tour operator can organize a visit and it's sometimes a venue on the Barbados National Trust's Open House Programme (see box, page 18)*, is in the old naval powder magazine of St Ann's Fort. It displays the majority of the **Barbados National Cannon Collection** (also known as the National Ordnance Collection of Barbados) and, with more than 400 great guns, is considered the world's rarest collection of 17th- and 18th-century English iron cannons. Some have royal seals from Charles II, Queen Anne, the King Georges and Queen Victoria. The most famous is the 1650 Commonwealth Gun, which bears the coat of arms of Oliver Cromwell – only one of two in the world (the other is in the Tower of London). A further 26 cannons from the National Cannon Collection can be seen in front of the Main Guard and clock tower looking on to the Garrison Savannah (page 35). The armoury also exhibits military memorabilia such as copies of old maps and colourful portraits of soldiers, and the tour includes a quick glimpse of the still-used 19th-century barracks. The late Mike Hartland, a major in the Barbados Defence Force, was the driving force behind the gathering of this unique collection, which was established in 2002. He found many of the guns from all along the west and south coasts of Barbados in gardens, cellars, on beaches, embedded in the sides of buildings and buried under fortifications.

ON THE ROAD
Beards and Bims – the naming of Barbados

Portuguese explorer Pedro a Campos 'discovered' Barbados in 1536 en route to Brazil and named it Los Barbados, meaning 'the bearded ones', and it is assumed this refers to the long, hanging roots of the bearded fig tree (*Ficus citrifolia*) found across the island. But it could have been the allegedly heavily bearded Caribs who once lived there, or perhaps the 'beard' of white foam created by waves breaking over outlying reefs that would have been seen by early sailors. Other names associated with Barbados are 'Bim', meaning a Barbadian person, and 'Bimshire' referring to the island. Bim could have been a corruption of the surname of Lieutenant General William Byam, a Royalist leader faithful to the Crown, who among many other Royalists fled to the Caribbean after being defeated by the Roundheads in the English Civil War. Following the execution of Charles I (1649), Barbados' government fell under the control of these Royalists, but in 1651, Parliament in England decided they would take back the island again and the Royalists were defeated by the British Navy. Byam was banished and went on to become governor of Suriname in South America, and his followers became known as 'Bims'. Another theory is that 'Bim' is derived from a word meaning 'my home' or 'my people' in the Igbo language of West Africa from the many slaves that arrived from modern-day southeastern Nigeria in the 18th century. Over time, and long before the island's independence, Barbados aquired the moniker of 'Bimshire', an affectionate reference to its long colonial relationship and Barbados being compared to an English county or 'shire'.

Charles Fort and around

To the west of St Ann's Fort, off Drill Hall Beach Road, and in the gardens of the **Hilton Barbados Resort** at Needhams Point (page 78), Charles Fort was built in 1650 and was the largest of the many forts which guarded the south and west coasts. Originally called Needhams Fort, the name was changed in 1660 when King Charles II regained the throne after Charles I was beheaded. In 1836 the fort was incorporated into the Garrison. Today, only the ramparts remain but there are a number of 24-pounder cannons dating from 1824 pointing out to sea, and there is a good view across Carlisle Bay. Between the Hilton and St Ann's Fort, the **Military Cemetery** dates back to 1780; the headstones make interesting reading – it appears, for instance, that disease claimed more lives than military action. Visible only from the beach to the south of the Hilton, the disused **Needhams Point Lighthouse**, octagonal in shape, was built in 1855. When it was in use, it had a half-red, half-green stationary light that let approaching vessels know if they were port or starboard of Carlisle Bay.

Around Bridgetown

a handful of historical and natural sights

Harry Bayley Observatory

Observatory Rd, Clapham, St Michael (about 4.5 km west of central Bridgetown), T622 2000, www.hbo.bb, Fri-Sat 1900-2200, Sun 1830-2200, US$13, children (5-12) US$5, under 5s free. To *get there take Bay St/Highway 7 and then turn off on to Beckles Rd and then Brittons Cross Rd and the observatory is on the left.*

In the Clapham residential area and named after Dr Harry Bayley, a brilliant Barbadian physician and keen amateur astronomer who founded the Barbados Astronomical Society in 1956, the observatory is open to the public at weekends (weather permitting). Built in 1963 (and refurbished in 2014), it is the only observatory in the Eastern Caribbean and is a chance for northern visitors to look through a 16-inch reflector telescope at the southern hemisphere stars and planets, which aren't all visible from North America and Europe. The moon, Jupiter and Saturn can all be seen on a cloudless night.

St George Parish Church
Highway 4B, The Glebe, St George, about 8.5 km northeast of central Bridgetown, T429 0371, see Facebook. Open daily 0600-1800, free but donations appreciated.

After the original church dating from 1637 was destroyed in the hurricane of 1780, another, built on the same site four years later, survived the next great hurricane of 1831 and remained intact during those of 1898 and 1955, making it the oldest ecclesiastical building on the island. Inside there is a magnificent altar painting of the Resurrection by Benjamin West, the first American president of the Royal Academy, a post he held from 1792 until his death in 1820. King George III was a patron of Benjamin West and many of his paintings hang in Buckingham Palace. There are also marble sculptures by Richard Westmacott, the creator of the statue of Lord Nelson in National Heroes Square, Bridgetown.

Gun Hill Signal Station
Gun Hill, Fusilier Rd, Newbury, St George, T429 1358, www.barbadosnationaltrust.com, Mon-Sun 0900-1700, US$8, children (under 12) US$5.

A five-minute drive from the St George Parish Church heading uphill, the approach to Gun Hill is by Fusilier Road where you will pass the white lion carved by British soldiers in 1868, before turning left to the signal station. This road was built by Royal Scot Fusiliers between September 1862 and February 1863 when they were stationed at Gun Hill to avoid contracting yellow fever. The signal station itself was initially constructed in 1816 when it was decided that a military presence would be maintained outside Bridgetown in case of slave uprisings. The strategically placed hexagonal tower was one of a chain of six signal stations across the island that were also used to communicate news and

> **Tip...**
> The view from Gun Hill is one of the most expansive on the island, taking in the whole of the south coast across to Bridgetown harbour.

messages using flags and lantern codes. Today Gun Hill is maintained by the Barbados National Trust and houses a collection of military memorabilia, although the real reason to come here is to enjoy the incredible view. Informative guides will explain the workings of the signal station and point out interesting features of the surrounding countryside. There is a small café with tables on the lawns called **Fusiliers**.

National Botanical Gardens
Waterford, St Michael, T536 0592, daily, free.

Located on the northern outskirts of Bridgetown, a stone's throw from the National

Stadium, the recently created National Botanical Gardens offer a serene escape from the hustle and bustle of everyday life. From the moment they set foot through the gates, visitors are transported to a world of soothing sounds and lush vibrant colours, not least of which the dazzling yellow-and-orange national flower known as Pride of Barbados. There are also many fruit trees, including a magnificent grove of mango trees. But it's not only plants that offer delight to the visitor here, for in the rainy season natural pools attract a variety of gorgeous birds. The site particularly comes alive at weekends, with locals bringing picnics and the kids flying kites.

The gardens first opened in 2019 and are still very much in development, with just one-third of the 101 ha site having so far been landscaped and developed at the time of writing. The government's Reclaiming Our Atlantic Destiny (ROAD) programme has recently secured US$75 million in funding from the Development Bank of Latin America and the Caribbean, part of which is earmarked to pay for the construction of an amphitheatre at the National Botanical Gardens to host cultural events, performances and festivals.

Overlooking the gardens are the dramatic ruins of Codrington House, which dates to 1825, and which was originally home to a local agriculturalist called John Redman Bovell, who now features on the Barbados two-dollar banknote. A US$10 million renovation project began in 2023 with the aim of restoring many of this historic building's original architectural features.

Tropical Garden Barbados (formerly Orchid World)

Groves, St George, T433 0306, https://tropicalgardenbarbados.com, daily 0900-1600 usually but check website for closure days, US$15, children (5-13) half price, under 4s free. The Sergeant St bus from Fairchild St Bus Terminal, Bridgetown, stops outside the entrance.

Located between Gun Hill and St John's Church on Highway 3B in St George, more than 30,000 orchids are grown in this 2.4 ha (6 acre) garden in a beautiful, mind-blowing display; don't miss this. They come from all over the world, and are grown on the ground in full sun, on trees, in coconut shells, are trained on wire fences so their roots don't touch the ground, and in 'houses' for partial shade under nets. A path meanders down the hillside, initially through woodland and past a waterfall, where orchids and other plants grow in their natural environment. Then you come out on to lawns where the path is directed between living fences of orchids, before you are bombarded with visual splendour in the orchid houses. There's a gazebo which offers a panoramic view of the valley and sugar cane fields, and a snack bar and gift shop selling images of orchids on tea towels, trays, mugs and numerous other souvenirs. There are also plants for sale.

West coast

Known as the Platinum Coast with luxury wall-to-wall low-rise hotels and villas along the seafront, the west is not just for posh pensioners and well-heeled celebrities. Good-quality cheaper accommodation can also be found if you are prepared to walk a few minutes to the beach. The strip starts just north of Bridgetown: Brandons Beach, within the confines of town, comes first, and then as you head up the west coast you will come to the main tourist area around Holetown, Speightstown and up to Little Good Harbour. Everything is accessed from Highway 1, which is easily drivable – though always busy with traffic – and well served by buses. Highway 2A runs parallel inland, goes through the sugar cane heartland and gives access to a number of tourist sights. Most of the west coast is lined with golden sand, and even the towns of Speightstown and Holetown have tempting beaches which are clean and attractive. All beaches are public, but access can be tricky where there is solid development and some hotels and restaurants block you out by denying access or cramming the sand with their sunbeds; look out for footpaths between hotels where you can get down to the water. The beaches are narrow and often eroded, but all have west-facing sunset views and the sea is usually calmer here than elsewhere.

Bridgetown to Holetown
a busy stretch of upmarket hotels including one of the world's most prestigious resorts

Brandons Beach and Brighton Beach
Just north of Bridgetown off Mighty Grynner (Spring Garden) Highway and about a 2 km walk from the Bridgetown Cruise Terminal is **Brandons Beach**, which has a car park, a changing facility with toilets and showers, and lifeguards, and is busy at weekends with families from Bridgetown. The main attraction here is the **Rascals of Barbados Waterpark** ⓘ *T234 9999, www.rascalswaterpark.com, daily 1000-1800, adults US$25 per hour, children (6-16) US$17.50 per hour, no under 6s.* This is a state-of-the-art inflatable aqua waterpark off the beach – a concept that's becoming very popular across the Caribbean and Rascals is considered the largest. Reached by a pier, it features giant interconnecting inflatable slides, jumps, trampolines and obstacles, and two different sides – a junior line on the inside and an outside ocean line for all ages. The excellent beach bar and restaurant has a good choice of cocktails and Bajan food, and weekly specials like Sunday lunch and a Friday 'after work lime' with DJ (check the Facebook page). Two sun loungers and one umbrella cost US$20.

Brighton Beach, just north of Brandons Beach, is very similar (car park, changing facilities and showers, sun loungers, umbrellas and lifeguards). At the northern end the 'Hot Pot' is a pool of warm water in the sand, created by a nearby power plant that pumps extremely hot water out to the ocean. Local people like to soak in it and it is clean and relaxing, but great care should be taken as there can be a strong undertow; don't swim close to the outlet pipe, and check conditions before jumping in.

Behind Brandons Beach is the **Mount Gay Visitor Centre** ⓘ *Exmouth Gap, off Mighty Grynner (Spring Garden) Highway, St Michael, T227 8862, www.mountgayrum.com, Mon-Fri 0900-1700, Dec-Apr Sat 1000-1600,* where you can learn all about and taste Barbados' historic rum (the distilleries themselves are in the northern part of the island). Mount Gay's roots can be traced back to the first production of sugar cane on the island, and the oldest surviving deed for the company is from 1703, making **Mount Gay rum** the oldest rum and longest continually produced spirit in the world. Today several varieties are produced including **1703**, **Silver**, **Black Barrel**, **Extra Old** and the flagship **Mount Gay Eclipse**. There are four tours to choose from: the one-hour Signature Tasting Tour does not require pre-booking and includes an introduction and tastings (tours depart hourly, Mon-Fri 0930-1430, Dec-Apr Sat 1000-1430, US$28). Book ahead for the Cocktail Workshop (US$68), Tastings & Lunch (US$83) and the Distillery Tour (in St Lucy, from US$60).

Batts Rock and Paradise Beach
About 1 km north of the roundabout where Highway 1 begins, turn sharp left. Drive down to **Batts Rock Beach** and walk south to get to **Paradise Beach** via a concrete path through a shady wooded area and alongside the sprawling and now derelict Four Seasons hotel development that stalled around 2009. Batts Rock has a car park, children's playground, picnic tables, showers and changing facilities. There is a lifeguard station at Batts Rock but none at Paradise Beach. Both beaches are lovely and quiet and, thanks to calm water and shallow rock formations, snorkelling is good and turtles often accompany you.

Paynes Bay
The heart of the Platinum Coast, Paynes Bay is a wide sweep of pale golden sand with trees at one end and crystal-clear water for swimming. It's a 20-minute stroll from end to end, and the northern half, away from the hotels, is usually uncrowded. There are

ON THE ROAD

Turtles

Barbados attracts a large number of hawksbill turtles, and smaller numbers of leatherback and green turtles. Adult females typically return to the beaches near where they themselves hatched in order to make their own nests and lay their eggs. The hawksbill and green nest between May and October, mainly on the west and south coasts of the island, while the leatherback, the largest of all turtle species, nests between February and July on the windswept beaches of the east and southeast coasts. Hawksbills can often be spotted playing and feeding along the inshore reefs and at snorkelling spots on the south and west coasts, and, during the nesting season, visitors to these coasts have a good chance of seeing at least one nesting hawksbill during a two-week stay. A very popular activity, particularly with children, is to go on a boat trip and swim with them as they feed among the coral. A long history of hunting these animals for their meat, eggs and shells has massively reduced Caribbean populations. However, turtle hunting and the possession of turtle products is illegal on Barbados and the **Barbados Sea Turtle Project** (*www.barbadosseaturtles.org*) has carefully monitored turtle activity since 1984. During the nesting season, staff patrol high-density nesting beaches at night; when necessary they relocate nests that are too close to the high tide line, and rescue hatchlings disoriented by hotel lights or turtles that have been accidentally hooked or partially drowned in fishing nets. The project provides a 24-hour year-round **Sea Turtle Hotline** (*T230 0142*), which the public and visitors can use to call in information on nesting turtles, hatching of eggs, exposed eggs in the sand, or lost or injured turtles. Additionally, you can call the hotline if you are interested in witnessing the release of hatchlings or watching the teams tagging the females, or if you want to make a donation (the project relies heavily on sponsorship).

---

shower and changing facilities, sun lounger and umbrella rentals, lifeguards and plenty of restaurants and beach bars in this area. Watersports are available from several outlets on the beach and activities include jet skis, kayaks, boogie boards, inflatable doughnuts, banana boat rides and catamaran cruises. Everything is very casual and relaxed, although expect a little harassment by beach vendors. Snorkelling is good here as the little reef directly in front of **Treasure Beach hotel** has colourful marine life and is quite close to the shore, and there are many buoyed-off areas. The green and hawksbill turtles are usually further out, roughly 250 m offshore; you need to be a strong swimmer and it is open water with jet skis and speedboats zooming by. It is safer to go out on a glass-bottomed boat; you can then swim around the boat with snorkelling gear. The going rate is around US$30 per person for about an hour. The best time to visit the turtles is either early in the morning or late in the afternoon when they often approach and

Tip...

There are several points of access through the resorts to the beach at Paynes Bay but parking is limited. Try the roadside just south of Sandy Lane where the trees give shade and a path leads down to the beach; otherwise park a bit further south. Plenty of buses stop on Highway 1.

ON THE ROAD

Sandy Lane

Backing on to the arc of golden sand at Sandy Lane Bay between Paynes Bay and Holetown, **Sandy Lane** (*T444 2000, www.sandylane.com*) is an institution on Barbados. You can't miss it as you drive up Highway 1, passing its grand entrance through the gracious avenue of ancient trees on the sea side of the road and the golf course on the inland side. It first opened in 1961 after Ronald Tree, a former British politician, had an idea to build a luxury hotel and golf course on what was an old sugar plantation named 'Sandy Lane' (his own beach house, **Heron Bay**, could no longer accommodate all the rich and famous people who wanted to stay there). With just 52 rooms, it quickly became known as the most elegant and sophisticated hotel on Barbados – indeed, at that time, in the Caribbean. As such it attracted a wealthy clientele that included film stars, politicians, royalty and dignitaries, all fleeing winter in the northern hemisphere for a spot of pampering in the tropical sunshine. There was a change of ownership in 1996 after which the hotel was closed for several years. It reopened in 2001, having been rebuilt rather than refurbished. The hotel's new owners had just one goal in mind: to recreate the most distinguished address in the Caribbean but to elevate the hotel to a whole new level in line with modern expectations in the super-luxury resort market. Today it's the sort of place where butlers unpack for you and beach attendants polish your sunglasses and make sure there isn't a grain of sand on your towel. No expense is spared: everything – from an underwater sound system in the vast swimming pool, to golf carts kitted out with GPS – is designed with luxury in mind. The atmosphere is plush and, while the place is packed with celebrities in the peak winter months, it's full of normal people (albeit very well-heeled ones) at other times. The 112 plantation-style rooms range from vast to palatial, and rack rates start from US$1500 per night in low season and become stratospheric in the winter high season. Golf has always been a big thing at Sandy Lane, and there are three courses; the hotel has a desalination plant for watering the greens and fairways and keeping the five manmade lakes full. The Old Nine nine-hole course dates from 1961 and the two newer 18-hole courses, **Country Club** and **Green Monkey**, were designed by Tom Fazio. If you can't afford to stay, an opportunity to see the place is to go and eat there, but you have to book ahead to get past the gate. The two main restaurants both have a great reputation and are in stunning open-air beachfront locations. Pillared and romantic L'Acajou offers fine dining, while the more informal Bajan Blue is known for its afternoon tea (1500-1700) and indulgent buffets, including a Sunday brunch (1230-1500).

are quite curious; from around 1000 until 1300 is when the large catamarans come into the bay and there can be hundreds of people in the water.

About 2 km inland from Paynes Bay Beach on Holders Hill is **Barbados Polo Club** (page 95), and on the same property is the beautiful **Holders House**, which overlooks the Old Nine golf course at Sandy Lane. A traditional Bajan plantation house dating from the 17th century with an elegant, wrap-around veranda and set in 2 ha (5 acres) of formal parklike gardens with a long meandering driveway, it is available as a house rental (six bedrooms and a state-of-the-art music studio; T244 5400, see Facebook or Airbnb). It also hosts the **Holders House Farmers Market** every Sunday in the grounds (page 92).

Holetown

modern town bursting with restaurants and a good sandy beach

Holetown in St James, the island's third-largest town, boasts a large selection of restaurants, nightlife and shopping. Today it's a thoroughly modern town but it was originally named Jamestown, after King James I of England, and is the place where Captain John Powell landed in 1625 and claimed the island for England. Two years later, on 17 February 1627, his brother Captain Henry Powell landed with a party of 80 settlers and 10 slaves. The Holetown monument commemorates these events although it gives the incorrect date. A secondary plaque correctly marks the 350th anniversary of the first permanent settlement in 1627. The settlement was, until 1629, the island's only town, and it had the first fort and first governor's house. Holetown acquired its name because of the offloading and cleaning of ships in the very small tidal channel near the beach known as the 'hole'. After Lord Carlisle gained control of Barbados as a protectorate of the Crown, he decided to found his own settlement, which became Bridgetown, in the southern part of the island.

Sights

There is public beach access down paths near the post office and the police station on the main road (parking is behind the police station and bus stops are along Highway 1). The sand is swept every morning while the early risers are jogging or walking their dogs along the West Coast Boardwalk (a concrete path along the beachfront), and beach operators offer a range of watersports as well as sun lounger and umbrella rental. Holetown is overloaded with restaurants and bars, and even with a two-week stay here you'd be pushed to try them all. Most of them are along First Street and Second Street – the first two streets to be built on Barbados and today the main nightlife area on the west coast.

Holetown provides the main shopping outside Bridgetown. On Highway 1 at the junction with First Street is the **Limegrove Lifestyle Centre** ⓘ *T620 5463, www.limegrove.com, Mon-Sat 1000-1800, restaurants later*, an attractive and upscale four-storey complex built around three open-air courtyards, which has luxury designer outlets, art galleries, restaurants, a spa and **cinema complex** (page 92). On the main road opposite the post office is a large branch of the **Massy Stores** supermarket ⓘ *T432 1127, www.massystoresbb.com, Mon-Sat 0800-2000, Sun 0900-1600*, and next door to the south and set in lovely tropical gardens is the **Chattel Village** ⓘ *T432 4691, Mon-Sat 0900-1700, Sun 0930-1300*, a group of replica traditional fretwork chattel houses (see box, page 21), all brightly painted, containing boutiques selling handicrafts, souvenirs and beachwear, a gourmet food shop and a couple of cafés. About 800 m south of the Chattel Village, the **Bridgetown Duty Free Sunset Crest Shopping Mall** ⓘ *T539 4400, www.bridgetowndutyfree.com, Mon-Sat 0830-1730, Sun 1000-1500*, stocks an impressive range of duty-free items including liquor, designer clothing and swimwear, perfume and cosmetics. During the **Holetown Festival** in February (page 13), the roadside along this stretch of Highway 1 is crammed with people attracted by an open-air market for arts and crafts, helped along with tempting local food and drink, while the road itself becomes a parade ground.

Legend Garden Condos **12**
Little Arches Boutique
 Hotel **13**
Little Good Harbour **14**
Lone Star **15**
Magic Isle Beach
 Apartments **16**
Manderley Villas **17**
Nautilus Beach
 Apartments **18**
O2 Beach Club & Spa **19**
OceanBlue Resort **20**
OceanSpray Apartments **20**
The Rockley by
 Ocean Hotels **21**
Round House **22**
The Sandpiper **23**
Southern Palms
 Beach Club **24**
Sugar Cane Club **25**
Time Out Hotel **26**
Tropical Sunset Beach
 Apartment Hotel **27**
Yellow Bird Hotel **28**

Restaurants
Bliss Café **1**
Café Sol **2**
Champers **3**
Cariba **4**
East Point Grill **5**
Fisherman's Pub **6**
Fusion Rooftop **7**
Harlequin **2**
Just Grillin **8**
The Mews **7**
Naniki **9**
Naru Restaurant
 & Lounge **10**
The Sea Shed **11**
Surfers' Café **12**
Tapas **13**
The Tides **14**
Zemi East Coast Café **15**

St James Parish Church

Highway 1, north end of town, over the bridge on the left, T422 4117, daily 0700-1730, Sun services 0715, 0800, 0900. This, the oldest church on the island, was presumed to be established when the first settlers arrived in Holetown in 1627. However, the exact date of the original church is not clear although records held by the British Museum state that 'The Hole Church' on Barbados had been in existence well before 1668; there are also references to the church made in both 1629 and 1660. It is known that the original wooden building was destroyed by a hurricane in 1675 and was replaced by a light coral stone structure in 1680. In 1874, columns and arches were added and the nave roof raised. You can see the original baptismal font (1684) under the belfry, and in the north porch is the original bell of 1696. Many of the original settlers are buried here (although the oldest tombstone of William Balston, who died in 1659, is in the Barbados Museum). There are several photos of registers, with many deaths attributed to the smallpox epidemic of 1695-1696. The lovely stained-glass window depicting the Ascension was dedicated in 1924 in memory of the fallen in the First World War. On the front pew is a plaque to the ex-President of the USA Ronald Reagan and his wife Nancy, who worshipped here on Easter Sunday in 1982.

Folkestone Marine Park and Museum

Highway 1, opposite St James Parish Church, T536 0648, daily 0900-1700, free entry. This marine park stretches 2 km from Sandy Lane Bay in the south to the area known as Church Point; **Dottin's Reef** lies just offshore and is enclosed by buoys for snorkelling. The reef is not in pristine condition but it is surprisingly rewarding as there are quite a lot of fish and other marine life such as sea anemones, sea lilies, corals and sponges, and you may see hawksbill turtles. Further offshore there is an artificial reef created in 1978 by the sinking of the Greek freighter SS *Stavronikita*, which rests under 36 m of water and is now home to numerous schooling large fish and corals. Because of its depth, and the fact that it is large enough for divers to get lost inside, the *Stavronikita* is classed an intermediate- to experienced-level dive (for dive operators, see page 93). The beach is not great at Folkestone but it is always crowded with people taking advantage of the safe swimming and snorkelling in the cordoned-off sea. Weekends are busy with families bringing enormous picnics and barbecues, cheerfully setting up home around a picnic bench. For around US$25 per person, glass-bottomed boats take you over the reef to two smaller wrecks further down the coast. The small two-roomed **museum** ⓘ *Mon-Fri 0900-1700, US$3, children under 12 US$2*, features displays and a photographic exhibit on marine life. Other facilities include a basketball court, children's playground, snack bar, toilets, showers, changing rooms with lockers and lifeguards; snorkelling gear can be hired. If you come by car there is a good shady car park, but you can also walk along the beachfront from Holetown, partly on the sand and partly on the West Coast Boardwalk.

East of Holetown

some varied outdoor excursions including a fantastic botanical garden

East of Holetown there is a clutch of attractions either side of Highway 2, also easily reachable from Bridgetown. Many of those listed below are in close proximity to each other in the island's central hillier and cooler parishes of St Thomas, St Joseph and St Andrew, and make a pleasant day trip away from the beach.

★ Welchman Hall Gully

Welchman Hall, St Thomas, off Highway 2, T234 9960, www.welchmanhallgullybarbados.com, daily 0900-1600, last entry 1530, Nov-Apr free guided tour Mon-Fri at 1030, other guided tours available with 24 hrs' notice, US$15, children (5-12) US$8, under 5s free.

Welchman Hall Tropical Forest Reserve, more commonly referred to as the Welchman Hall Gully, is in St Thomas, one of the hilliest parishes on Barbados. The gully was formed by the collapsed roofs of caves and is a fascinating 30- to 45-minute walk through one of the deep ravines that are so characteristic of this part of Barbados. You are at the edge of the limestone cap which covers most of the island to a depth of about 100 m. Owned by the Barbados National Trust, the site has recently

> **Tip...**
> To get to Welchman Hall Gully from Bridgetown, Transport Board bus No 4 (to Shorey Village) goes every hour from the Princess Alice Bus Terminal, and also stops at Harrison's Cave Eco-Adventure Park 1.4 km before the gully (*www.transportboard.com*).

been enhanced with interpretive signage and new guided and self-guided walks on good paths, most of which are wheelchair-friendly. The first section has a devil tree, a stand of bamboo and a Judas tree. Next you will go through jungle, which has lots of creepers, the 'pop-a-gun' tree and bearded fig clinging to the cliff (note the stalactites and stalagmites); a section devoted to palms and ferns – golden, silver, Macarthur and cohune palms, nutmegs and wild chestnuts; to open areas with tall leafy mahogany trees, rock balsam and mango trees. At the end of the walk are ponds with lots of frogs and toads. Best of all though is the wonderful view to the east coast. On the left are some steps leading to a gazebo, at the same level as the tops of the cabbage (royal) palms. Look out for green monkeys, which are very likely to make an appearance thanks to banana feeding between 1030 and 1200. Entry fee to Welchman Hall Gully includes a booklet that lists over 50 plants and trees, and there are clear and informative signs along the walk. There's a children's playground with a tree-house, mini zip line and rope swing.

Harrison's Cave Eco-Adventure Park

Allen View, St Thomas, off Highway 2, T417 3700, http://chukka.com/barbados/harrisons-cave-eco-adventure-park, daily 1 hr tram tours 0845-1545, many pricing combinations including tram tour only US$59, tram & dinner show US$125, gully challenge course US$55, zip line US$70, cave exploration tour US$99, tram, trail & zip line US$129, tram, trail & rum experience US$139, all-inclusive adventure pass US$179. Free pick-up & drop-off from your hotel included with most passes.

Welchman Hall Gully is connected geologically to nearby Harrison's Cave, about 1.4 km to the south. It's named after Thomas Harrison who was the landowner in the early 1700s, although it wasn't officially explored or mapped until 1974. Long known for its tram tours of the limestone caverns, Harrison's have recently expanded their offering with an eco-adventure park that includes a nature trail, interpretation centre, aviary, zip line, swimming pool, rum-tasting experience, restaurant and bar. There is also an impressive visitor centre, gift shop, and a small display of local geology and Amerindian artefacts. The cave tour, which showcases superb stalactites, stalagmites, waterfalls and underground lakes, takes around an hour and includes stops for photo opportunities – but be prepared to get a bit wet as the caves drip.

On Highway 2 heading towards Bridgetown you will pass **Jack-in-the-Box Gully** (and the road of the same name) on the left about 3 km south of Harrison's Cave. Part of the same complex as the cave and Welchman Hall Gully, it was also formed by the breaking off of the limestone cap in the area, and another natural rainforest has developed within it. **Coles Cave** is an 'undeveloped' cave (no gate or entrance fees) that lies at the north end and is usually accessed from Highway 3A. It has beautiful caverns adorned with stalactites and stalagmites, an underground stream, and rock pools in which to splash around or even swim depending on water levels. With sturdy shoes and a torch it can be explored independently, or Grantley from **Good Times Tours** ⓘ *T241 4067, see Facebook*, is a renowned local guide for a two-hour tour with headlamps, refreshments and transport from US$100 pp (minimum 2).

Mount Hillaby

About 2 km northwest of Welchman Hall Gully via Canefield Road is Mount Hillaby, or Hillabys as it is affectionately called by Barbadians, the highest point on the island at a modest 337 m. It lies in the Scotland District in the parish of St Andrew, although the village of Hillaby borders St Andrew and St Thomas. It's not a pointy-topped mountain, more of an extended ridge of about 4 km. A narrow and pretty winding road goes up from the village though cattle farms and sugar cane fields to the top, where a small trail and steps into the bush lead to a concrete summit marker. If you visit Mount Hillaby early in the morning you'll most likely see the area covered in an enchanting mist. Later in the day the mist clears to reveal broad views of the lush countryside to the northeast coast. To reach the village from the west or south, go via Highway 2A and then Duke's Road.

Coco Hills Forest

ⓘ *Richmond Road, St Joseph, T571 5520, see Facebook. Daily 1000-1600, US$12.50, children (6-12) US$6, not suitable for small children, 2 hr guided farm tour and hike at 1000 and 1400, US$25.*

Up Richmond Road just under 2 km northeast of Welchman Hall Gully are two delightful attractions close to each other, although you'll need a car/taxi as they are difficult to access by public bus. Coco Hills Forest is midway up Richmond Road and is a privately owned 20.2 ha (50 acre) forest used as part of an agroforest and organic farming project. What initially began as a venture for owner Mahmood Patel to grow coconuts and greens for the café at his Ocean Spray Apartments (page 85) on the south coast, it's now a wonderful destination for short hikes. This green oasis features bamboo groves and hundreds of royal palms and primordial tree ferns, and growing in the forest are coconuts, bananas, mangoes, coffee, cocoa and pineapples, and numerous herbs and spices. Around 2 km of trails fan out from the entrance and you can either strike out on your own or take a guided tour to learn about the indigenous flora of Barbados. Green monkeys are present, and from the highest point at 300 m there are expansive views of the east coast.

★Flower Forest Botanical Gardens
Richmond Rd, St Joseph, T433 8152, www.flowerforestbarbados.com, daily 0800-1600, US$15, children (4-12) US$7.50, under 4s free. To get there turn off Highway 2 on the Melvin Hill road just after the agricultural station and follow the signs.

Just 300 m beyond Cocoa Hills Forest at the end of Richmond Road, and at 270 m above sea level, is this 21 ha (53 acre) beautifully landscaped botanical garden on a former sugar plantation. Named paths wend their way around the hillside; they are well maintained and even suitable for wheelchairs, although there are a few which go off the beaten track and can only be negotiated on foot. The garden contains species not only from Barbados but from all over the world, all beautifully arranged with plenty of colour year round. You can find heliconias, ginger lilies, orchids, anthuriums, ixoras and bougainvilleas as well as productive plants such as bananas, cocoa, coffee and breadfruit. The outstanding feature of this garden, however, is the forest. Enormous trees loom above you, with royal and other palms giving shade to the paths, while in

> **Tip...**
> A good map/information sheet is provided for a self-guided tour, umbrellas are available if it's drizzly, and there's a pleasant café for lunches and teas.

between you can find bearded fig trees, huge baobab and mango trees. Here and there they open on to large grassy areas affording excellent views over the valley to the east coast. **Liv's Lookout** in particular has a fantastic outlook all up the northeast seaboard. To the west you can see Mount Hillaby (page 51).

Hunte's Gardens
Castle Grant, Highway 3A, St Joseph, T417 3700, www.huntesgardens-barbados.com, daily 1000-1600, US$20, children (6-12) US$7. From Bridgetown's Fairchild Street Bus Terminal, Transport Board bus No 5C (Chalky Mount) goes hourly and drops in Sugar Hill, from where it's a 1 km walk east on Highway 3A to the garden.

Along Highway 3A at Castle Grant is another treat for keen gardeners, Hunte's Gardens, which can easily be combined with visits to Welchman Hall Gully and the Flower Forest Botanical Gardens. This rainforest garden was created from the 1950s by horticulturist Anthony Hunte in a gully, with flowering plants growing in a variety of habitats, from sunny, open spaces to a dark sinkhole. A pretty path winds its way through a series of little gardens tucked away in private areas with strategically placed benches where you can pause to admire the view and watch the birds and butterflies. Species identification leaflets are provided, and at the end you can enjoy a rum punch, teas, coffees and homemade cakes on the veranda of the main house.

Speightstown and around
characterful town known for its original buildings and laid-back charm

The coastal Highway 1 runs north from Holetown on to Speightstown in the parish of St Peter and 22 km north of Bridgetown. This is the second-largest town on the island and the bus terminus for the north, but, with a population of less than 4000, it retains a village atmosphere with street vendors selling fresh fruit and vegetables and fishermen unloading their catch along the jetty. It is a lively place during opening hours, but dead the rest of the time. Pronounced Spikestown (or Spikestong), it is named after William Speight, a merchant and member of Governor Hawley's first House of Assembly. An important port in the early days, it was known as Little Bristol because of its trade with Bristol, England, and it used to have four jetties. It also had three forts, no longer in evidence: Orange Fort, Coconut Fort and Denmark Fort, while outside town were Dover Fort and Heywoods Battery. They didn't see a lot of action, but the town was once invaded by Oliver Cromwell's forces when Barbados remained loyal to King Charles I. Colonel Alleyne led the Roundheads ashore in December 1651, only to be shot dead by Royalists. His forces captured the town, their only victory, and a peace treaty was later signed at Oistins.

Sights
Speightstown has some interesting old buildings, once-grand town houses that belonged to the wealthy merchants, and many two-storey shops with Georgian balconies and overhanging galleries. Sadly many have been knocked down by passing trucks and several restaurants and other buildings were lost to a fire in 2020 – though not as devastating as an earlier fire in 1941 that destroyed almost everything near the bridge on the ocean side of **Queen's Street**. This area was replaced with the **Speightstown Esplanade**, a pleasant waterfront with a stage area and wooden bench seating for outdoor events, and a tremendous view along the town's coastline and beaches to the south. Just south of the Esplanade is the **Speightstown Fish Market** (flying fish is one of the most popular catches, but also look out for marlin, kingfish, mahi mahi, swordfish and tuna; ask the vendors what's in season). Alongside the fish market's long jetty is the characterful, if not slightly ramshackle, rum shop-style **Fisherman's Pub** (page 87), which has been owned by the same family since it opened in 1939; with a great view of the sea from the terrace, it is a popular local watering hole and lunch stop for tourists on island tours.

Arlington House Museum ⓘ *Queen's St, T422 4064, www.barbadosnationaltrust.com, daily 0900-1700, US$15, children (5-17) US$8, under 5s free.* Arlington House is a 17th-century 'single house', meaning it's the width of a single room. It is believed to have been the prototype for the Charleston Single, common in Charleston, South Carolina, but is the last remaining example on Barbados. It tapers towards the back and the ground-floor room was once believed to have been a chandler's, as the original owners, the Skinners, owned one of the town's jetties. There is a separate entrance to the first-floor room and above that there is a second floor with a balcony, the main living quarters for the family and, above that again, an attic with gabled windows that was probably used for sleeping and storage. The house was built of coral, limestone and rubble masonry, all cemented together with a mortar made from egg-whites and molasses, creating walls that are over two feet thick. It has been beautifully renovated by the Barbados National Trust as the Arlington House Museum, with audiovisual displays including videos of interviews with members of the local community. It's very engaging and exhibits are well arranged under three subjects: **Speightstown Memories** introduces the lives of the island's first settlers; **Plantation Memories** illustrates the influence of colonization, the plantation system and the sugar cane industry on the island; and **Wharf Memories** recalls the importance of Speightstown as a leading port and trade hub.

St Peter's Parish Church ⓘ *Orange St, T422 3599, see Facebook, Mon-Fri 1000-1800, Sat 1000-1300, Sun services 0730, 0915, 1900.* First built of timber in 1629, then again in 1665, St Peter's was rebuilt once more in 1837 in early Georgian style with an impressive square bell-tower and ramparts. The architecture was strongly associated with the number seven, relating to the seven days of Creation in Genesis I: there are seven windows to the north and south, seven columns in the interior, the roof is divided into seven parts and the stained-glass window has seven sections. A fire in 1980 destroyed the roof and floors, although the fine eastern stained-glass window and the walls survived. The church was restored in 1983. Visitors are made very welcome at Sunday services and the choir is quite wonderful.

> **Tip...**
> St Peter's Parish Church's Annual Flower and Garden Festival is a five-day event held every January, when the best floral arrangers of the island showcase their talent and the church is decorated with blooms such as anthuriums, heliconias and orchids (see Facebook for details).

The Speightstown Mural An unusual attraction in town is a *trompe l'œil* ('deceive the eye' in French) mural depicting the history of Barbados in its many phases. Privately commissioned in 2013 by restaurateur Pierre Spenard, it is on the north wall of Jordan's Supermarket between the seafront and Queen's Street. It measures 21 m by 7.5 m, and was painted by Bajan artist Don Small and Californian John Pugh, who is known for his large murals with three-dimensional scenes, and took 18 months to complete. The detail is fantastic and the longer you look at it, the more you see of the people and events that have created modern Barbados. Scenes of Harrison's Cave blend seamlessly into historical scenes of the raising of the Barbados flag at independence, while green monkeys merge with chattel houses and the original Amerindian inhabitants of the island.

Just below the mural on the town's beach that runs between Jordan's Supermarket and Fisherman's Pub is a chic little beach bar: **One Eleven East Beach Bar** ⓘ *T537 0459, see Facebook, Tue-Thu 0900-1900, Fri-Sun 0900-2100,* offers sun loungers, comfy sofas, booze and coffees, sandwiches, pastries and a chalkboard menu of specials. It also rents out stand-up paddle boards and kayaks and is a perfect spot for sunset-watching.

Mullins Beach and Gibbes Beach The 275 m-long stretch of soft white sand at **Mullins** is just south of Speightstown off Highway 1B. It shelves gently into usually calm water and has roped-off areas for snorkelling and swimming. As well as a large car park, there are sun loungers and umbrellas for hire, plenty of shady trees, and vendors offering watersports, although there are no changing facilities or lifeguards. There has been some erosion of the beach so it's narrow, but it is still a lovely place to come for the day. A shack behind the beach sells beer, rum and ice creams, while **The Sea Shed** (page 86) is a stylish upmarket beach bar and gourmet restaurant, and a great spot to watch the sun set. Immediately south of Mullins Beach is **Gibbes Beach**, an entirely uncommercialized arc of pristine sand, backed by soaring trees and some of the most desirable villas on the island. There are no loungers or umbrellas for rent, and little shade from the trees after around 1300, but it's a much quieter spot than other beaches on the west coast. The drop-off into the sea can be quite steep so keep an eye on small children. If you're willing to get your legs wet, you can sometimes reach Gibbes by walking around from Mullins (it depends on the tide); otherwise it's a tricky track through the villa properties down from Highway 1B. Both beaches are well served by local buses.

North of Speightstown

A glitzy 9 ha (22 acre) marina has been built at Heywoods Beach just north of Speightstown. Known as **Port St Charles** ⓘ *T419 1000, www.portstcharles.com*, it is a huge and impenetrable development with a massive wall around the outside to deter casual visitors. It is also an official port of entry into Barbados with coastguard, police and immigration on site for entry by yacht or helicopter. Arranged around a small inland manmade lagoon, there are 145 residential villas, condos and apartments, restaurants, a yacht club, heliport and watersports, as well as berths for around 140 yachts including six superyachts (up to 250 ft in length). Water taxis scoot around the lagoon taking residents to the various facilities on site or on shopping trips to Speightstown. Most of the apartments and villas are privately owned, but some are available for short-term holiday rental. Public access to Heywoods Beach is off Highway 1B between the all-inclusive **Almond Beach Resort** and Port St Charles, where there is a small road and parking. The water at this quiet beach is calm and good for swimming and snorkelling, and there are some small rock-enclosed pools that are perfect for children to wade in. There are lifeguards but no facilities (the sun loungers are for hotel guests only); bring everything you need.

Immediately north of Port St Charles, Highway 1B passes through Six Men's fishing village on the bay of the same name. The picturesque beach lines a long row of small homes, rum shops, wooden boats and palm trees, but has mixed sea conditions and some undertow; it is mostly used by local fishermen serving the tiny fish market and the odd Bajan surfer. Divers, however, may want to explore the *Pamir*, a 165 ft wreck of a freighter that was scuttled in 1985 to create an artificial reef that lies only 30 m offshore in **Six Men's Bay**. Easily accessible by boat or swimming from shore, and with many large holes in its hull, it's a popular spot for first-time wreck divers.

North of Six Men's, Highway 1B turns inland towards the parish of St Lucy in the north of the island, while the **Sherman Hall Moon Fort** coastal road, lined with simple chattel houses, is generally quiet, except when buses come whizzing through. The unkempt sandy beach along this stretch has a certain charm but backs on to the road and can be narrow at high tide; there are rocks underwater and it is predominantly used for hauling up fishing boats. Nevertheless, around the village of Sherman are a clutch of exclusive villas and the **Little Good Harbour** hotel, where **The Fish Pot**, one of the best restaurants on this part of the coast, is a good spot for lunch (page 86).

North coast

Far from the crowds and the bustle of the west and south coasts, the northern tip of Barbados in the parish of St Lucy has a rugged and picturesque landscape of dramatic coral limestone cliffs, jagged rock formations, and quiet, isolated bays. The true 'north' begins after Port St Charles, and soon you leave behind the development of the west coast strip and emerge into proper countryside as Highway 1B veers inland. Narrow roads lead off to the coast. The Atlantic Ocean can be rough and wild and huge waves crash into cliffs, creating tunnels, caves, platforms and enormous jacuzzis. Round the tip on the eastern side there are some lovely shingle coves to explore and, away from the popular picnic spots, it's deserted. Swimming is possible at low tide but be cautious, and take local advice about which places are safe and which have dangerous currents. The northeastern part of the country is known as the Scotland District for its rugged appearance and similarities perceived by the first colonizers. Although the landscape doesn't match the majesty of the Scottish Highlands, it has its own charms and there are some interesting places to explore.

Along the north coast

a wild coastline where Atlantic waves crash against cliffs

Animal Flower Cave
North Point, St Lucy, off Highway 1C, T439 8797, www.animalflowercave.com, Tue-Sun 0930-1600, US$20, children (under 12) US$10; restaurant 1100-1530.

Located on the rugged and ragged clifftops of the northernmost point of the island is this expansive cave, one of many caverns created by the pounding waves of the Atlantic, with its mouth above the sea when it is calm. The 'animals' are sea anemones but, while they were seemingly in abundance when the cave was discovered and named in the 1700s, they are rarely seen today. A stairway through a blowhole in the bedrock provides access, and guides will walk you through several huge chambers filled with beautiful rock formations, some of them tinted by the oxidation of copper and iron, and take you to rock 'windows' just above the level of the sea. Wear good shoes as the coral floor of the cave is uneven and can be slippery, and bring swimming gear as there is a totally transparent and absolutely still pool in one chamber where you can swim looking out to sea. The views over the cliffs and ledges are dramatic, especially when the winter swells arrive, and there's an excellent restaurant with a deck to watch the Atlantic crash into the rocks below. The menu offers Bajan specialities; recommended options include salted cod fishcakes, slow-roasted ribeye, and breadfruit tacos – quite delicious and all you'll need for lunch – while on Sundays a fuller menu includes blackbelly lamb stew.

> **Tip...**
> Buses from Bridgetown go via the west coast and Speightstown to Connell Town on Highway 1C; tell the driver to drop you at the end of 'Cave Gap' and from there it's a 10-minute walk along Animal Flower Cave Road.

Ladder Bay and River Bay
Rounding the northern tip of the island, you will find several remote coastal areas to visit: Ladder Bay, River Bay, Little Bay and Cove Bay. Some of these coarse sandy coves, popular with Barbadians for picnics at the weekend but otherwise completely deserted, are only accessible along tracks. There are good walks along the cliffs around here; for instance, from Ladder Bay to River Bay and on to Little Bay along the Antilles Flat. But beware, as the ground is rocky and there is no shade; wear sturdy shoes and sun protection.

The abandoned and now-ruined North Point Surf Resort at **Ladder Bay** is off Highway 1C. Park outside the wall, from where you can walk around the **Spout**, a geyser-like 30 m-high water spurt courtesy of a spectacular blowhole, and a small, rather dangerous beach. Just south, at **River Bay**, there's a shallow, calm spot to take a dip while the Atlantic rages a few metres beyond. It has a public changing facility with showers and toilets, and is served by the odd bus from Connell Town; an option here would be to combine a visit with the Animal Flower Cave and walk between the two (which takes about an hour) and then catch a bus from either side.

Little Bay and Cove Bay
If you drive inland from Ladder Bay and then through Spring Garden, you'll re-emerge on the coast at **Little Bay** near the village of Pie Corner. There is a quiet beach here with golden sand and limestone cliffs, usually unoccupied unless a tour group stops by. The sea here is far too perilous for swimming, but on the north edge of the bay there's a ledge of rock protecting a completely circular and calm natural pool that is just deep

enough to swim in. Pick your way over the jagged rocks carefully and wear shoes. You can also climb up the cliffs overlooking Little Bay for a good view of the north coast's spectacular blowholes.

A bit further south and in a peaceful, rural setting, **Cove Bay** (also called Gay's Cove) is a popular picnic area and very scenic. It's not easy to get to and while you can drive to the cliffs overlooking the bay, the track goes through a field of cows, goats and blackbelly sheep. It is easy to get bogged down so if the ground looks wet, park further back on Cove Bay Road and walk the last kilometre or so. From the clifftop vantage point you get a good view of the semicircular bay below (it's a bit of a scramble to get down to the shingle beach itself), and beyond it to the 80 m-high **Pico Teneriffe**, a large rock on top of a steeply sloping cliff. The whole of the coast to Bathsheba is visible too, lined with the foam of breaking Atlantic waves.

Inland from the north coast

a great house, sugar plantations and indigenous island wildlife

Just inland from the northeast coast are a group of attractions that are fairly close to one another and are easily accessed via Highway 2A from Bridgetown and the west coast, or Highway 2 from the east coast. Spanning the parishes of St Peter and St Andrew, this region is the hilliest area of Barbados and there are plenty of views across to the coast and the Scotland District.

★ St Nicholas Abbey

Cherry Tree Hill, St Peter, T422 5357, www.stnicholasabbey.com, Sun-Fri, 1 hr abbey and distillery tours 1000-1630 (last tour 1530) and visitors must depart the property by 1700, US$35, children (3-14) US$12, under 3s free.

St Nicholas Abbey is on a 162 ha (400 acre) estate comprising 91 ha (225 acres) of sugar cane fields as well as lush tropical gullies, mahogany forests, formal gardens and **Cherry Tree Hill** (260 m), a prominent landmark that you can walk or drive up, or catch the train (see below). If you're going south and inland from Cove Bay it's just under 4 km via Boscobelle; other routes to the abbey from the west coast and the south go via Highway 2A; there are plenty of signposts.

Approached down a long and impressive avenue of mahogany trees, St Nicholas Abbey was never actually an abbey – it has no monks' cells or cloisters and some have supposed that the 'St' and 'Abbey' were added to impress. It is, however, one of only three surviving Jacobean mansions in the western hemisphere (the other two are Drax Hall, also on Barbados in St George near the centre of the island, the first place on the island where sugar was cultivated in the 1640s and today a private residence; and Bacon's Castle in rural Virginia in the USA which, like Barbados, was a wealthy English plantation colony in the 17th century). St Nicholas Abbey is thought to have been built by Colonel Benjamin Beringer in 1658, but was sold to Sir John Yeamans, who set out from Speightstown in 1663 to colonize South Carolina. The three-storeyed house has a façade with three ogee-shaped Dutch gables over its main portico and cornerstone chimneys and fireplaces of local coral stone; as these are unnecessary in the Caribbean it's likely that Beringer purchased the plans in England.

Today, scrupulously restored, it is one of the architectural treasures of Barbados, with a Chippendale staircase and cedar-panelled rooms containing antique furnishings including a 1759 James Thwaite of London grandfather clock, an 1810 Coalport dinner service and a collection of early Wedgwood portrait medallions. Visitors are given an interesting tour of the ground floor of the house, as well as the rum and sugar museum and the gardens. The rum distillery uses a traditional pot-still to make the unique St Nicholas Abbey Rum sold in the shop, which also sells molasses and brown sugar from the estate, plus jellies and chutneys made with fruit from the gardens. Behind the house, near the 400-year-old sandbox tree, the **Terrace Café** serves lunch, tea and other light refreshments.

From the top of Cherry Tree Hill there are glorious views all over the Scotland District, which falls mainly within the parish of St Andrew. It is believed that cherry trees grew here once, but today the road up the hill is lined with mahogany trees.

The **St Nicholas Abbey Heritage Railway** ⓘ *T572 1999, https://snahr.com, US$35-70, children (3-14) US$12-24, under 3s free, daily (except Sat in Apr-Nov) 1000, 1130, 1400, 1445*, runs from the station just inside the main gate of the abbey, where there's also a small coffee shop. It's a gentle-paced and very scenic 3 km train ride in open carriages pulled by a diesel or steam locomotive. In particular, railway enthusiasts will enjoy seeing Tjepper No 5, built in Germany in 1914 before being shipped to Java, Indonesia to work on sugar plantations, and spending later life in the UK's steel and coal industries. After extensive restoration it arrived on Barbados in 2019. The railway follows a route past St Nicholas Abbey, around an ornamental lake and through woods and plantations to the top of Cherry Tree Hill. It takes around an hour with a break at the top to enjoy the views, and if they wish, passengers can assist the staff with turning around the locomotive on a turntable for the return journey.

Morgan Lewis Sugar Mill
Morgan Lewis, St Peter, T622 4039, Tue-Sat 1100-1600, US$3 pp entry to the mill, grounds free.

At the bottom of Cherry Tree Hill, about 2.5 km south of the abbey, the Morgan Lewis Windmill was built around 1776 and was the last working sugar windmill on Barbados; it stopped operating in 1947 and in 1962 was given to the Barbados National Trust. The mill consists of a tower with housing on top, four giant arms, gears that transfer the turning of the sails to the turning of the rollers, and a 33 m tail that connects the housing to the ground. By moving the tail, the whole apparatus could be rotated to face the direction of the prevailing wind, and it's one of only two sugar mills in the Caribbean with its equipment all intact (the other is at Betty's Hope Estate in Antigua). However, sadly it no longer functions as lightning struck and disabled the tower in 2007. But you can explore the interior exhibiting plantation artefacts and old photographs, climb partway up into the mill to see the machinery, and relax afterwards at the adjacent Mosaic at the Mill Café which offers nice countryside views from the outside tables.

Barbados Wildlife Reserve and Grenade Hall Forest and Signal Station
Farley Hill, Highway 2, St Peter, T422 8826, daily 1000-1700 (last entry 1600), US$15, children (3-12) US$8, under 3s free.

This family attraction off Highway 2 occupies 1.6 ha (4 acres) near the top of Farley Hill, next to the Grenade Hall Signal Forest and Signal Station. It was first established by a Canadian primatologist in 1982 for the conservation and study of green monkeys, which arrived on Barbados in the 17th century on slave ships from West Africa and are now widespread on the island. Short paths meander through the mahogany forest, where banana trees and other fruit and vegetables are planted to feed the animals. Some of the paths are steep and quite uneven but, if you look closely at the bricks, you can still see the stamps of the British manufacturing companies; the bricks were brought to Barbados as ballast on ships during the 17th and 18th centuries and used to construct boiler furnaces in sugar factories; now they have been recycled as these pathways.

Animals seen roaming all over the paths include the bushy-tailed mongoose, peacocks, guinea fowl, tortoises, iguanas and the large red-footed Barbados tortoise, while brocket deer and agouti lounge in the shade to escape the heat. The caged birds and reptiles are less impressive (the parrots particularly seem frustrated). It is, however, an excellent place to see green monkeys close up if they haven't taken off to the forest next door. The best time to come (especially for children) is for the 1100 and 1400 feeding when staff bring out wheelbarrows of fruit, the monkeys return and other animals gather expectantly. Try to be quiet, so as not to disturb them. A café and shop at the reception area sell snacks, drinks and gifts.

The entry fee to the reserve also covers Grenade Hall Forest and Signal Station next door, where winding shaded pathways with interpretative signs have been laid out through the whitewood, dogwood, mahogany and silk cotton trees; some are steep and slippery so watch your footing. The signal station (1819) was one of six erected at strategic points across the island for communication using flags or semaphores (to warn of such things as approaching ships or slave rebellions). Today it has been restored and an audio guide gives the history with sound effects. The wonderful panoramic views give you a good idea of its original role in the communications network.

Farley Hill National Park
Farley Hill, Highway 2, St Peter, T422 3555, daily 0830-1730, free for pedestrians, US$3 per car to park.

On the other side of the road from the wildlife reserve and set in a pleasant park popular with Barbadian families for Sunday picnics is the atmospheric ruin of Farley Hill House. Building began in 1818, with additional rooms being added over the next 50 years. It eventually grew to be regarded as the most impressive mansion on Barbados and in the mid-19th century the property was owned by Sir Graham Briggs, a wealthy British planter and legislator, who improved both the house and gardens, importing many plants and trees on to the island. It was used as the location for the 1957 film *Island in the Sun* – the story of a love affair across racial boundaries, starring Harry Belafonte and Joan Fontaine. Sadly, in 1965, a disastrous fire destroyed the house's interior and roof, and only the solid stone walls survived. It was purchased by the government and was opened as a national park by Queen Elizabeth II in 1966. Now, if you look through the mahogany trees and across a manicured lawn, you'll see the imposing Georgian stone façade pierced by great windows; benches have been set at strategic points so you can enjoy the breeze coming in off the Atlantic and the spectacular views over the Scotland District, right down to the lighthouse on **Ragged Point**. There are many imported and native tree species, some labelled, planted over 7 ha (17 acres) of woodland, and the forest is transformed into the stage for musical and theatrical events several times a year. It is also a popular venue for weddings.

Tip...
To get to Farley Hill for both the national park and the Barbados Wildlife Reserve and Grenade Hall Forest and Signal Station, take any bus along Highway 2 and get off at Benny Hall, St Peter; everything is signposted and the bus driver will tell you where to alight.

East coast

Wild and windy, unspoilt and untamed, the Atlantic coast has a raw energy and is stunningly beautiful. Craggy cliffs form a backdrop for huge bays filled with boulders which appear to have rolled down the hillsides into the foaming surf. The strong currents and powerful waves make the sea too dangerous for swimming – Barbadians say 'the sea ain't got no back door' – but you can wade and look for sea creatures in the numerous rock pools and it is the nearest place to heaven for surfers, who can be seen out there at any time of day waiting for the right wave. Hiking is also excellent, particularly along the abandoned railway track which hugs the coastline. Some accommodation can be found in Bathsheba, the main village, but otherwise the east coast is sparsely inhabited, dotted only with colourful villages of wooden chattel houses and banana and coconut trees lining the roadsides.

Inland, but within easy reach of either the east or west coast, are several stunning gardens and natural attractions, such as ancient forests and caves.

Along the east coast
undeveloped and windswept, with stunning beaches and good walking

Much of the East Coast Road, opened by Queen Elizabeth II on 15 February 1966, has today been renamed the Ermy Bourne Highway. It runs from a junction with Highway 2 at St Andrew's Parish Church near Belleplaine, south through Barclays Park and Cattlewash and down to Bathsheba. Here it joins Highway 3, which branches off both southwest to Bridgetown and southeast through Bath to Codrington College and then beyond into the parish of St Philip. This drive, about 16 km from Belleplaine to the college, affords fine views of long beaches pounded by the Atlantic, while meadows tumble down from the hillsides into the ocean. Look out for grazing blackbelly sheep, which are commonly mistaken for goats.

St Andrew's Parish Church
Junction of Highway 2 and Ermy Bourne Highway, Belleplaine, St Andrew, T429 0703, services Tue 0700, Sun 0830.

Just under 3 km south of the Morgan Lewis Sugar Mill and 1 km before Belleplaine, this quaint but handsome English-style parish church on Highway 2 was first built of wood in 1630 and then reconstructed in stone in 1846 after being destroyed by a hurricane in 1831. It sits among lush casuarina trees and has a Gothic-style square tower and gallery running on three sides. Often locked except at service times, the grounds are lovely and the well-kept church with its white-painted gateposts, windows and gables is quite photogenic.

Turners Hall Woods
Isolation Rd, Cheltenham, St Andrew, just under 2 km west of Highway 2, open 24 hrs, free.

Inland of the Ermy Bourne Highway and southwest of Belleplaine are the 20 ha (50 acre) Turners Hall Woods. Although not well signposted (you may have to ask), they are reached by following Isolation Road; a distance of about 2.5 km from the highway. It is thought that these woods have changed little since the arrival of the English settlers, who stripped much of the island bare for planting sugar cane in the 17th century. There is a fairly steep main hiking trail of about 1.75 km, with several short secondary trails branching off to the left and right, and also a number of ponds and small streams flowing under the dense canopy of trees. At least 32 tree species have been identified, including silk cotton, sandbox, bulletwood, trumpet tree, locust, fustic and cabbage (royal) palms. About 152 cm of rain falls annually in this area, so it's not classed as a true rainforest, despite the multilayered tree canopy and the presence of lianas and ferns. But it can get very hot and humid in the forest, so take plenty of drinking water.

> **Tip...**
> Bus 1E links Speightstown on the west coast and Bathsheba on the east coast (50 minutes) via Highway 2 and the Ermy Bourne Highway; stops include Barbados Wildlife Reserve and Grenade Hall Forest and Signal Station, Farley Hill, St Andrew's Parish Church, Barclays Park, Cattlewash and Andromeda Botanic Gardens. Bus 6 runs between Bridgetown's Fairchild Street Bus Terminal and Bathsheba (50 minutes) via Highway 3.

Long Pond
Long Pond is a secluded coastal estuarine area about 1.5 km east of Belleplaine

off Ermy Bourne Highway; you'll need to park at Windy Hill and scramble a couple of hundred metres through the sand dunes to get there. It's a shallow brackish-water lagoon separated from the sea at low tide by a sandbank, and is fed by Long Pond River, one of the four rivers on the island. Thanks to crabs, tiny fish, shrimp and crustaceans, Long Pond is a habitat and foraging area for many shore and waterbirds including sandpipers, plovers and herons, and you may also see resident ospreys in the casuarina trees on the south bank of the lagoon. You can paddle but watch the very soft mud beneath your feet.

Barclays Park and Chalky Mount

About 2 km south of Long Pond at Benab, 20 ha (50 acre) **Barclays Park** straddles Ermy Bourne Highway and stretches from a wide swathe of dark tan-coloured beach on one side up the hillside on the other. Access is free, and it is a good place to stop for a picnic under the shady casuarina trees; there is parking on either side of the highway. The park was funded by Barclays Bank to commemorate independence in 1966 and was opened by Queen Elizabeth II. Above the park you can hike through meadows to the top of **Chalky Mount** for magnificent views of the east coast. It takes about 45 minutes to an hour, and if you ask locally for the exact path you are likely to be given several different routes. This 167 m-high hill of reddish-brown (not chalky) clay can be spotted from some distance away looming over the coast. Some people say it looks like the figure of a man resting with his hands over his stomach and it is also known locally as 'Napoleon'. In Chalky Mount Village (also accessed by road from the west side, bus 5C goes from Bridgetown's Fairchild Street Terminal), generations of potters living mostly in wooden houses on the hillside used to make local cookware such as 'pepperpots' (to preserve meat) and 'monkeys' (a kind of water jug). The practice has largely dwindled but **Chalky Mount Potteries** ⓘ *T422 9818, daily 0900-1600, demonstrations usually around 1200*, produces colourful glazed teapots, mugs, vases, lampshades and the like, and the studio's walls are decorated with lovely seascapes of ceramic fish, seahorses and turtles.

Cattlewash

On Ermy Bourne Highway between Barclays Park and Bathsheba, the long beach at Cattlewash is perfect for an isolated walk; the reef pools exposed at low tide provide safe waters in which to bathe and cool off. There is a lifeguard station manned at busier times but no other facilities. The beach got its name from the farmers who took their cattle there to be washed by the crashing waves to rid them of parasites. You can walk the 2 km from Cattlewash to Bathsheba along the sand.

★Bathsheba

Bathsheba is in the parish of St Joseph, about halfway up the east coast, and 19 km northeast of Bridgetown via Highway 3. It has a double bay with wave-eroded rocks and boulders at each end and in the middle. The beach is sandy but at the water's edge it turns to flat rocks, platforms interspersed with rock pools where you can cool off at low tide. Windswept and with pounding surf, swimmers confine themselves to these pools, best in the shelter of the enormous boulders (watch out for sea urchins), but Bathsheba is one of Barbados' top surfing beaches. The bay seems to be almost white as the surf trails out behind the Atlantic rollers. The popular surf spots are **Soup Bowl** and **Parlour**, where waves break consistently year-round but are best between September and November. Surfing championships are often held here. Bathsheba village is home to a small community of fishing folk and their families and is effectively just one long beach road, dotted with the odd rum shop; it's just about as laid-back as it gets on Barbados. If you're neither a surfer nor a tidal pool-paddler, then there

ON THE ROAD
Barbados Railway

Built in 1883, the 38.6 km (24 mile) Barbados Railway went due east from Bridgetown across the island, and then up the east coast to Belleplaine. It was built to transport sugar to the docks at Bridgetown for export, and also to afford Barbadians and visitors a luxurious trip to the east coast, where welcoming parties awaited them at hotels. The line had 98 bridges, severe curves and one of the steepest gradients of any railway in the world – the cutting at My Lady's Hole, near Conset Bay in St John is spectacular, with a gradient of 1:31. The railway had at its disposal five locomotives from England, named after the parishes through which the line ran. While the railway had some years of success, by the end of the 1800s it was plagued with many troubles. Firstly the train moved slowly, at an average speed of 6 miles (10 km) per hour, and had no washrooms; it is said that men could jump off the front of the train to relieve themselves, and jump back on the caboose afterwards. The railway took a beating from the Atlantic sea spray and from landslides and wave erosion, and the locomotives often slipped off the line; the crew would sprinkle sand on the track to get them back on again while the first-class passengers remained seated, the second-class walked and the third-class pushed. It continued to decay and by 1934 the service for passengers was discontinued; by 1937 the railway was shut down and the steel and tracks were removed altogether. Today there is a good hiking trail along the old railway line between Bathsheba and Bath.

are plenty of walks in the area. Low-key accommodation is available, and this is also where some Barbadians spend their weekends, with many owning holiday homes in the area.

Just south of Bathsheba (a suburb really), picturesque **Tent Bay** is home to a small fish market, and colourful local fishing boats can be seen making their way in and out of the bay in the morning and evening. Like the other beaches, there are strong currents and swimming is not recommended. The landmark **Atlantis Historic Inn** (page 82) opened here in 1884 when the old railway between Bridgetown and Belleplaine (1881-1937; see box, above) ran directly in front of the hotel and made a stop at the bottom of the steps. The **Atlantis** is still a great place for lunch on a tour of the island, and is well known for its Bajan buffets (page 87).

Hackleton's Cliff rises up in the woodland on the slopes behind Bathsheba and is one of the highest points on Barbados at about 1000 m above sea level. It was allegedly named after a man called Hackleton who committed suicide by riding his horse over the cliff in the 17th century. At the top of the cliff are three burial vaults dating back to 1865 and containing the remains of the Hackleton, Forster, Cox and Culpepper families, some of the earliest settlers to arrive on Barbados. On a clear day, it offers a tremendous view of the east coast spanning from Pico Teneriffe in the north to Ragged Point in the southeast. You can drive up to **Hackleton's Cliff Lookout** (with toilets and picnic benches) from the west side and Highway 3 via **Horse Hill**.

Andromeda Botanic Gardens
Foster Hall, Bathsheba, St Joseph, T248 0190, www.andromedabarbados.com, daily 0930-1630, last entry is at 1630 but exit whenever you wish, US$20, children (under 16) free with paying adults, entrance fee covers unlimited visits within 4 weeks.

Perched up on the hillside with a fabulous view of the ocean is one of Barbados' prettiest gardens. It covers 2.5 ha above the bay at Bathsheba and is within walking distance of the beach (although it is uphill all the way). The garden started as a private plant collection around the home of Iris Bannochie (1914-1988), a leading expert on horticulture on the island who laid out trails in 1954 alongside a stream, now a prominent water feature, on land owned by her family since 1740. She bequeathed the gardens to the Barbados National Trust in 1988. The gardens contain plants from all over Barbados as well as species from other parts of the world, particularly Asia, amounting to over 600 in total. Its blooms are regular winners at Chelsea Flower Show in the UK. You have a choice of two self-guided walks through immaculate gardens, sprawling over the hillside between limestone boulders – **Iris's Path** has more to see in the way of plants, while **John's Path** passes an astonishingly vast bearded fig tree. It is always full of interest and colour, with good explanatory leaflets for each walk, telling you of the uses of each plant as well as where to stop and rest. In 2022, an **ethnobotanical garden** was added, showcasing the relationship between local plants and Bajan culture, and two years later a wheelchair-accessible space called **Rochelle's Garden** opened to mark the gardens' 70th anniversary. The excellent **café** is open until 1645, and there's also an **art gallery**.

> **Tip...**
> Entry to Andromeda Botanic Gardens is free for UK members of the Royal Horticultural Society, and half price for members of the English and Scottish National Trusts.

St John Parish Church
Church View, St John, T433 5599, see Facebook, daily 0600-1800, Sun services 0700 and 0915, free but donations appreciated.

Around 5 km after Bathsheba on the way to Bath, turn off Highway 3 at New Castle and head inland for just over 2 km uphill to Church View and St John Parish Church (follow the road up from Martin's Bay on the coast). A classic solid Gothic church, it is in a magnificent location perched high up on a 240 m cliff with views over the Scotland District and the entire rugged east coast. The original church was probably built of wood around 1645, but it was destroyed by fire and was replaced in 1660 with a stone structure, which supposedly cost the diocese 110,000 lbs of sugar. The building was badly damaged by the hurricane of 1675, and successive buildings were destroyed by hurricanes in 1780 and 1831. The present church (the fifth) was built in 1836; the chancel was added in 1876 and its beautiful stained-glass windows were added quite a bit later, in 1907. There is an interesting pulpit made from five different kinds of wood – ebony, mahogany, manchineel, locust-oak and pine. You will also find the grave of Ferdinando Paleologus, a descendant of Emperor Constantine the Great, whose family was driven from the throne in Constantinople by the Turks. Fernando died in 1678, having been a resident here for over 20 years. There are some fine cabbage (royal) palms in the churchyard, which is interesting to stroll around, but pick your moment: the church is on the itinerary for island tours and you may be jostling for space with the occupants of the latest cruise ship in port.

Martin's Bay
On the opposite side of Highway 3 and down a steep twisty hill, Martin's Bay is a pretty beach perched below green-palmed hills. A shallow reef breaks the waves and creates small pools perfect for paddling; further out are rougher waters with lots of undertow, so stay close to shore. There's also a lawn for picnicking and a children's playground.

The rocky nature of the bay also makes it ideal for lobster fishing, and colourful boats bob around on the water. Great local seafood such as grilled or fried swordfish, marlin, red snapper and lobster (in season), with delicious sides like cassava, sweet potato pie, rice and peas, and green banana cou-cou, can be had at the local village rum shop/restaurant, **Bay Tavern** ⓘ *T433 5118, Fri-Wed 1000-1930, Thu 1200-1930*, which has picnic tables overlooking the bay, and on Thursday afternoon hosts a popular fish fry (or 'Thursday Lime') with DJ and music.

Bath

Around 7.5 km southeast of Bathsheba, with access off Highway 3, is the very pleasant beach and picnic spot at Bath. There are a few beach villas at one end, but otherwise this is an empty, unspoilt stretch with a long sweep of casuarina trees for shade. The sand is good but at high tide the sea covers it completely and you have to retreat into the trees. Low tide is wonderful with rock pools to wallow in for a lovely lazy day. Swimming is reasonably safe here because of an offshore reef, but you have to be careful of the rocks. Popular with Barbadians at weekends, when families pitch camp around a picnic table, it is deserted during the week and highly recommended for escaping the crowds. Facilities are good, with lifeguards, changing rooms with showers and toilets, and plenty of parking; a small snackette is open on busier days. Not only is there a children's playground, but there is also a large grass area for games such as football or cricket.

> **Tip...**
> The 5 km hike between Bathsheba and Bath along the coastal paths – parts of which follow the old railway line (see box, page 64) – takes two to three hours. You can stop for lunch at Bay Tavern in Martin's Bay, the halfway point. This isn't an overly strenuous hike, and the few hills that need climbing aren't very steep or high.

Codrington College

Sargeant St, St John, T423 1170, www.codrington.org, daily 0900-1800, US$2.50 per car for parking and access to gardens, entry to the historical buildings additional US$5, US$1 children (under 12).

Also in this area is Codrington College, one of the most famous landmarks on the island, which can be seen from the East Coast Road down an avenue of cabbage (royal) palm trees. Built in 1743, it is the oldest Anglican theological college in the western hemisphere, and the solid and dignified main building was patterned after an Oxford college. It is steeped in history as the first Codrington landed on Barbados in 1628. His son acted as governor for three years but was dismissed for liberal views. Instead, he stood for Parliament and was elected speaker for nine years. He was involved in several wars against the French and became probably the wealthiest man in the West Indies. The third Codrington succeeded his father as governor-general of the Leeward Islands, attempted to stamp out the considerable corruption of the time and distinguished himself in campaigns (especially in taking St Kitts). He died in 1710, a bachelor aged 42, and left his Barbadian properties to the Society for the Propagation of the Gospel in Foreign Parts. It was not until 1830 that Codrington College, where candidates could study for the Anglican priesthood, was established. From 1875 to 1955 it was associated with Durham University, England. Apart from its beautiful grounds and impressive façade, there is a chapel containing a plaque to Sir Christopher Codrington (Codrington the Younger) and a library. Visitors are welcome to stroll around the gardens, where there is a beautiful lily pond (the flowers close up in the middle of the day) stocked with fish and ducks, and there are picnic benches and a playground with a wonderful view of the Atlantic coast. You can follow the track which drops down 120 m to the sea at the beautiful **Conset Bay**, where there is a tiny fishing village with an exceptionally long jetty where fishermen bring in their catch.

Ragged Point

After Codrington College, another 7.5 km via Highway 5 takes you to the most easterly point of Barbados, Ragged Point, from where (on a clear day) there is a spectacular view along almost the entire east coast of the island up to Cove Bay and Pico Teneriffe. The name conjures up images of desolation, jagged cliffs and rugged rocks, which is exactly what you will find here, and the East Point Lighthouse, also known as **Ragged Point Lighthouse**, perches on top of the 27 m cliffs. It was built in 1875 at a height of 29.5 m and, now automated, stands among the ruined houses of the former lighthouse keepers. An atmospheric station close to the shoreline measures air quality; this is the first landfall after blowing across the Atlantic from the coast of Africa. Experienced surfers might want to try out the surf at Ragged Point, but access to the waves is by a difficult descent down the cliff face, which can be very slippery.

South coast

The south coast caters for the package holiday end of the market, with mid-range hotels packed in along the western end in districts with the charming English names of Hastings, Worthing and Dover, though there is little to distinguish them nowadays as the coast is entirely built up from Hastings to Oistins. The advantage of the south coast is that it is close to the airport and has better beaches, with wider expanses of sand gently sloping down to the sea. It is popular with families and a younger crowd and there are plenty of restaurants, shops and bars; lively St Lawrence Gap, known as just The Gap, is the main district for nightlife, while Oistins, a fishing village, sparks into life on Friday nights for a fish fry. The south coast is great for all sorts of watersports, but watch out for rip tides if you are swimming.

The southeast coast
good sandy beaches, a plantation house and a very famous aeroplane

The village of Six Cross Roads in the parish of St Philip is the main junction in the southeast – there are six roads extending from a central roundabout. From here Highway 6 heads towards Ragged Point and provides access to a number of beaches along this stretch of coast. In the southwest direction, Highway 5 goes from Six Cross Roads towards Oistins. There are also a couple of attractions within striking distance of the roundabout.

Sunbury Plantation Great House
6 Cross Rd, Marchfield, St Philip, T423 6270, www.sunburyplantation.com, Thu-Sat 0900-1600 (but liable to change, so best to call ahead or check their website), house tour (drink included) US$15, children (4-12) US$8, under 4s free. To get there, turn north on Highway 4B at Six Cross Roads roundabout, the plantation house is at the 1st T-junction; or take no 26 bus from Oistin's station.

One of the oldest houses on the island, Sunbury (pronounced Sun-berry) provides a fascinating insight into plantation life. It was built around 1660 from local rocks and ballast brought over in the ships from England and held together with a durable cement of limestone, sand, crushed coral and egg-white. Originally it had a fishpond roof for collecting water but this was damaged in the 1780 hurricane and was replaced in 1788. The Chapman family who built the house were among the first settlers and were related to the Earl of Carlisle, who had granted them land. Chapmans are mentioned on Richard Ford's map of 1674, which shows a cattle mill on the Chapman plantation. It changed hands and names several times, owned by the Brankers, Butler Harris and the Barrow family (who named it Sunbury after their home in England). One of the Barrow heirs was Colonel in Charge during Bussa's (slave) Rebellion of 1816, during which the plantation suffered damage valued at £4000. The estate never really recovered and in 1835 John Barrow sold up and emigrated to Newfoundland.

> **Tip...**
> The house has pretty gardens to enjoy, a gift shop, and a courtyard restaurant for Bajan lunches and English-style afternoon teas.

The new owners, the Daniel family, had made their money out of shipping sugar to England and owned several sugar estates, but they were absentee landlords. At the end of the 19th century, a Scotsman, Alistair Cameron, emigrated to Barbados, married a niece of the Barrows and in 1896 bought the estates of Sunbury, Hampton and Bushy Park after the death of Thomas Daniel. Two of the Cameron daughters remained living at Sunbury until their deaths in 1980 and 1981, when the land was sold to the estate manager. The house, which had been untouched for 100 years, was bought by Angela and Keith Melville, who, in 1984, opened the whole of Sunbury Plantation Great House as a museum. But in 1995 a fire swept through the upper floors destroying the old timbers, wooden floors and antiques, except for those in the cellar; however, the massive walls and a few floorboards were intact. A meticulous restoration was undertaken and the house reopened in 1996.

It is now again a museum and is crammed with a very busy collection of mahogany furniture, art, china and antiques. You can roam all over the house, and in the cellars you can see the domestic quarters with a good collection of old optical instruments and household items. There are also numerous carts and gigs, including one donated by Sir Harry Llewellyn, the British Olympic showjumper of the 1950s and 1960s.

Foursquare Rum Distillery
Four Roads, St Philip, T629 4500, www.rumsixtysix.com/foursquare, Mon-Fri 0900-1630 (no organized tours but you can visit at your leisure and there is a tasting room). Buses stop in Four Roads; ask the driver to tell you when you get to Foursquare (it's fairly obvious when you see the old sugar chimney).

Approaching from Six Cross Roads roundabout along Highway 6, you will see the large compound of the Foursquare Rum Distillery to the left. This is the most modern rum distillery on Barbados and is set on 3 ha (8 acres) of a former sugar plantation and factory dating back to 1636. The Seale family resurrected the defunct distillery in 1996, and it now produces several spiced rums including Doorly's and Rum Sixty Six, and the Exceptional Cask Selections have won many international awards. The tour here is usually run by entertaining manager Dario, who is passionate about rum (he mixes it into his porridge in the morning), and has exceptional knowledge about sugar production and distilling on Barbados. You'll also follow a route around the factory learning about the various stages of rum-making and seeing (and smelling) all the manufacturing processes. This is followed by a tasting session and bottles are available to buy at the Copper Still Bar; there's also a playground for kids while parents indulge.

★ Bottom Bay
Beginning just south of Ragged Point, the string of beaches on the southeast coast starts at Bottom Bay, 7 km east of Six Cross Roads via Highway 5, and 800 m from the highway down a turning at Apple Hall (buses can drop at this junction). This has to be the most beautiful beach on Barbados and one of the best in the Caribbean. What is more, it is often deserted, even in high season, but even with a few couples on the beach you will feel as though you've got the place to yourself. Steep cliffs surround the small bay and the sand is a glorious pale coral pink. You can park on the clifftop and then walk down steps carved between the cliffs on to a huge expanse of sand, where a clump of palm trees grows in true holiday brochure fashion. Sometimes there are boys on the beach who will offer to climb up to get coconuts down for you to drink the cool milk. There is a little hut under the coconut palms where you can usually hire sun loungers and umbrellas, but it is not always open midweek or in low season. The only shade is under the palm trees or the cliffs, but with few other people around, that is usually plenty. The sea is often rough with quite big waves, better for jumping and splashing about than swimming. This area is becoming a popular part of the island to live in, and many new homes are being built on the clifftops. While there are no hotels in Bottom Bay, some places are available as holiday rentals. A short walk south along the cliff from Bottom Bay overlooking Cave Bay are the ruins of **Harrismith** plantation house that was built in 1920 and was once a hotel. You can park near this building; a long flight of stone steps carved into the cliff leads down to the beach. Also known as **Harrismith Beach**, Cave Bay has no facilities, and the strip of sand is narrower

Tip...
The No 12A Transport Board bus from Fairchild Street Bus Terminal in Bridgetown follows the entire south and southeast coast via Hastings, Rockley Beach, Worthing, St Lawrence Gap, Maxwell, Oistins, Grantley Adams International Airport, Foul Bay, Crane Beach, Sam Lord's Castle, Long Bay and Apple Hall (for Bottom Bay), ending in Merricks. Other buses do shorter sections of this route too: www.transportboard.com.

ON THE ROAD
The Gentleman Pirate

Stede Bonnet (1688-1718) was an unlikely Barbadian pirate because he was a wealthy landowner of a 400 acre estate southeast of Bridgetown. For some unexplained reason, and despite his lack of sailing experience, he abandoned his wife, children, land and fortune, and turned to piracy in 1717. It was rumoured he had marital problems, or he may have been having financial issues due to his sugar cane crop being wiped out by a hurricane or another natural disaster, or perhaps it was the worst mid-life crisis of the 18th century. He bought a sloop with 10 guns, which was unusual as most pirates seized their ships by mutiny or converted a privateer vessel to a pirate ship. He named it *Revenge* and recruited a pirate crew of 70 and, in another break from tradition, paid his crew wages, not shares of plunder as most pirates did. Bonnet ran up the Jolly Roger and set off on the high seas, capturing other vessels in a series of colourful escapades along the Eastern Seaboard of what is now the United States. In Nassau, Bahamas, then known as the 'pirates' republic', he partnered with Edward Teach, better known as Blackbeard, the most famous and feared pirate of his day. Together they made several raids along the New England coast. Bonnet's downfall came when the governor of South Carolina commissioned Colonel William Rhett to capture him. In August 1718, Rhett cornered the *Revenge* at the mouth of the Cape Fear River and, after a violent firefight, managed to capture Bonnet and his crew. Bonnet tried to take advantage of his upper-class background by appealing to the governor for mercy and blaming everything on Blackbeard. But he was hanged on 10 December 1718, after less than two years of adventure, and just a month after Blackbeard had met his own bloody end in battle with the British Royal Navy. With his stylish clothes and powdered wig, Bonnet had stood out among the bearded, unkempt, ill-mannered pirates with whom he sailed, and he was often referred to as the 'Gentleman Pirate'.

than that at Bottom Bay, but palm trees grow behind the beach for shade and there is a lagoon formed by a reef, which gives protection for bathers.

Long Bay

The next beach to the southwest is on Long Bay, a glorious stretch of pink sand separated into three coves by cliffs with wooden steps going up from one beach and down to the next. Two of the bays front the former **Sam Lord's Castle**, once the home of a notorious pirate who wrecked ships visiting the shores of the southeastern coast. Samuel Hall Lord (1778-1844) reputedly hung lanterns in the trees to look like the mouth of Carlisle Harbour and lure ships on to Cobbler's Reef where they were shipwrecked. There is said to be a tunnel from the beach to the castle's cellars. The proceeds made him a wealthy man although the 'castle', a regency mansion built in 1820, was probably financed by his marriage to a wealthy heiress who later left him and fled to England. Another legend tells of how the captain of one of the wrecked ships murdered Sam Lord in London in 1844. In the 1970s, the castle was converted to a luxury hotel, attracting royalty and film stars, but it gradually declined until it was abandoned in 2003. Then in 2010 a mysterious fire gutted the once-magnificent building leaving only the shell. The castle and surrounding property were eventually leased by the Barbados government to the Wyndham Hotel Group, and construction of a lavish 422-room resort was started in 2017. It stalled several times, but finally opened in 2024. Blending modern elegance with this historical site awash with pirate legends, the new upscale all-inclusive resort (see page 80) offers spacious ocean-view suites, half a dozen swimming pools, a full-service spa, fitness centre, kids' club, and several superb restaurants and bars. The beach is now private access for guests only, but anyway the sea here can be rough and unpredictable with strong undercurrents and rip tides.

A better place to swim is the **Shark Hole**, about 400 m south of Sam Lord's Castle in a residential villa area. This is a tiny patch of pretty beach, at its widest no more than about 12 m across, which heads a little spoon-shaped bay with the sea coming in through a narrow funnel in the low coral cliffs. It's protected from the full force of the waves by a coral ridge, so at low tide is a sheltered and unusual place to wade and swim. By contrast, it's dangerous during high tide when the waves cause a vicious rip. There are no sharks, but the natural pool may have been named by a local fisherman called Sharky.

Crane Beach

Crane Beach is another fabulously deep beach with plenty of powder soft coral pink sand and vibrant turquoise water. The waves are a bit rough for swimming but very popular with boogie-boarders and great for splashing about and generally having fun. Sun loungers, umbrellas and boogie boards can be hired on the beach and there are lifeguards. The **Crane Resort** (page 82) is perched on top of cliffs at the southern end of the beach. It opened in 1887, making it the oldest continuously operating hotel on the island (although most of the resort buildings today are modern blocks and timeshare apartments). In the 18th century there was a crane on the top of the cliff for loading and unloading ships, hence the name. Even if you are not staying there, the resort has an excellent choice for dining including L'Azure Restaurant, which offers a great buffet breakfast (daily 0730-1100) with an eagle's-eye view of the bay before you descend to the sands. The resort also has a shopping mall, **The Crane Village** – a reconstruction of a traditional Barbados town with cobbled streets, gas lamps and wooden shuttered windows – where shops include a supermarket, boutiques, jewellers and a branch of Bridgetown Duty Free. There's also the casual Italian **D'Onofrio's Trattoria**, **The Village Café** for ice cream, pastries and coffees, and **Bar 1887** for cocktails.

If you park at the resort they will charge you access through their grounds (with a glass elevator or steps down to the beach), redeemable against a drink at the bar or meal at one of the restaurants. Alternatively, carry on to a little roundabout and turn down a narrow lane which leads to a car park where stepping stones give access to the southern end of the beach.

> **Tip...**
> Just before the public beach access path, and bright yellow so hard to miss, is **Cutters Bajan Deli** (*T423 0611, www.cutters.bb, daily except Tue 1100-1800, dinner by reservation only 1800-2000*), which offers excellent fish cutters (sandwiches) plus other light meals and deli items to eat in or take away. Alternatively, you can pre-order a picnic or lunch which is delivered to you on the beach. You can also pre-book a two-hour 'Rum Punch Masters Mixology Class' for US$50 per person including lunch and a 750 ml bottle.

Foul Bay

Just south of Crane Beach, on the other side of the roundabout, is Foul Bay; if driving, take the turning down Foul Bay Road to a car park. This is the longest beach on this part of the coast with large cliffs at each end and idyllic pink sand with turquoise water. It's wide and open and less crowded than Crane Beach, but sea conditions are similarly rough with a strong undertow where the waves break. There are no lifeguards, so be cautious about swimming, if at all. Despite this, it's ideal for picnics and isolated walks, and has some shade under casuarina and palm trees, a few tables and benches, toilets and showers.

The southwest coast
the main beach resort area with hotels and apartments lining the coast

The southwest coast is a string of beautiful expanses of white sandy beaches backed by hotels, bars and restaurants, within striking distance of Grantley Adams International Airport and where public transport is readily available. It's not as glitzy as the west coast, nor is it as expensive, but it is popular with package holidaymakers and has all the facilities they may need for some fun in the sun.

Enterprise (Miami) Beach

Off Highway 7 just southeast of Oistins is this 230 m-long beach, also known as Miami Beach. This very attractive and popular beach is in two parts, divided by a lifeguard station between the two bays. The western side offers calm waters ideal for wading and swimming (even for children), while the eastern side has occasional swells, especially at high tide; avoid swimming near the coral rocks at the end, and the general

> **Tip...**
> Many buses travel from Bridgetown along the Highway 7 south coast route to Oistins and beyond; get off at the Oistins Post Office stop and follow the pathway from there about 250 m to Enterprise Beach.

rule everywhere is to stay within your depth. Lots of Barbadians come here, especially at the weekends, and early morning or before sunset for a stroll, jog or dip in the sea. There's plenty of shade under casuarina and broadleaf trees and everything you could need for a pleasant day on the beach, including sun lounger and umbrella rental, toilets, showers, picnic tables and vendors selling beach towels and sarongs. The legendary **Mr Delicious Snack Bar** ⓘ *T233 3354, see Facebook, open until late most nights*, is an old yellow bus that offers excellent fish cutters, rum punch and lemonade; catamaran tour parties often anchor here for lunch.

From Enterprise Beach there is a good view of **South Point Lighthouse**, the oldest lighthouse on Barbados, which was reassembled on the southernmost point of the island in 1852, one year after being shown at London's Great Exhibition. It is 27 m high and painted with thick horizontal lines of red and white. The grounds (but not the tower) are open to the public; follow the signs through the residential area of **Atlantic Shores**, just to the east of Enterprise Beach.

Oistins

Oistins, the main town in the parish of Christ Church, is 8 km west of Grantley Adams International Airport. It was named after plantation owner Edward Oistin. After the execution of King Charles I in 1649, Barbados declined to acknowledge Oliver Cromwell

ON THE ROAD
★ Oistins Fish Fry

Held at Bay Gardens near the fish market, Oistins Fish Fry is a major street party on a Friday night for both Barbadians and tourists. Busloads of tourists are ferried in from resorts around the island and it's a lot of fun. Excellent flying fish, as well as tuna, swordfish, barracuda, kingfish, marlin, mahi mahi and lobster, plus pork chops, ribs and chicken, with sides of coleslaw, green salad, baked macaroni pie, rice and peas and hot sauce, are all served in an extremely informal setting from about 30 or so wooden stalls and eaten at communal bench tables. It attracts hundreds of hungry people and food is usually available from around 1800. There's also plenty of drinking, as well as karaoke, steel pan bands, and live calypso and reggae on the main stage area for dancing. For a big plateful of food, expect to pay in the region of US$15, and about US$3 for a bottle of Banks beer and US$6 for a rum punch. A smaller event happens on Saturday night, and on other nights many stalls do food and some bars are open, but it is low key and mostly caters for locals liming and playing dominoes.

and his commonwealth parliament. This resulted in six months of resistance to Cromwell's fleet in 1651, which led to the signing of the 'Articles of Agreement' in a tavern called the 'Ye Mermaid's Inn' in Oistins on 11 January 1652. This was later acknowledged as the Charter of Barbados by the Parliament in England. Oistins Beach is divided into two bays, separated by rocks and the jetty. It is now the main fishing port on the south coast, with colourful boats pulled up on the shore. The Oistins Fish Market is worth visiting, even if you don't want to buy, to see the expert skill and lightning speed with which the women fillet flying fish and bag them up for sale. The **Fish Festival** is held over the Easter weekend celebrating fishermen's skills with demonstrations of fish boning, boat racing and crab racing, helped along with steel pan music and dancing.

The **Christ Church Parish Church** ⓘ *Church Hill Rd, T428 8087, www.christchurchpc.com, Mon-Fri 0930-1700, Sun services 0700, 0930*, overlooks the town (a bit of a steep walk up) and is the fifth parish church to be built on the site. The original was constructed in 1629 and that and subsequent structures were all destroyed by natural disasters including flood, fire and hurricanes. The present Anglican church was built in 1935 and has an impressive barrel-vaulted ceiling, a fine stained-glass altar window and is flanked by a large, wooded graveyard which is notable for containing the Chase Vault. When the vault was opened in 1812 for the burial of Colonel Thomas Chase, the lead coffins were mysteriously found scattered around inside. It happened again in 1816, 1817, 1819 and 1820, whereupon the coffins were removed and buried separately in the churchyard. Whatever had been moving them around had thrown them about with such violence that the wooden coffin of Mrs Thomasina Goddard (1807) had smashed to splinters and taken a chunk out of the vault wall. To this day no conclusive explanation has been given for this bizarre occurrence.

Welches Beach and Maxwell Beach

West from Oistins, Highway 7 runs right along the edge of **Welches Beach**, which is quiet and wide with a nicely landscaped boardwalk. However, there are no facilities here including sun lounger and umbrella rental or lifeguards, so swim with caution as the sea can be rough at times with some undertow.

Highway 7 veers inland slightly and a turn-off about 350 m down Maxwell Coast Road (ask buses to drop you here) takes you to **Maxwell Beach**. It has lovely coral-white sand and the water is fairly calm, even for supervised small children. There are several hotels in the Maxwell area (including the vast property at the western end occupying the adjacent all-inclusive adults-only resorts of Sandals Barbados and Sandals Royal Barbados) so the beach can get busy, but there is still plenty of space and it's long enough for a good walk. Several watersports can be arranged including banana boat and inflatable doughnut rides, Hobie Cats and jet-skiing. You can rent sun loungers and umbrellas, and the woodland area adjacent to the car park has picnic tables under shady trees and there are toilets.

Dover Beach and St Lawrence Gap

Between Maxwell and the southern end of the popular tourist area of St Lawrence Gap, **Dover Beach** is a beautiful horseshoe-shaped bay lined with hotels and with pristine white sand and turquoise water: picture-postcard stuff. It's a great place for lazing around, sunbathing and cooling off in the sea, which is usually calm and protected and there's a lifeguard station. On the beachfront is a timber boardwalk, with numerous stalls selling everything from drinks, ice creams and snacks to suntan lotion, hats, T-shirts, beachwear and snorkelling gear. Picnic tables are scattered around the beach, sun loungers and umbrellas can be rented, and kayaks, Hobie Cats, boogie boards, windsurfers and jet skis are available.

'The Gap', as **St Lawrence Gap** is usually called, begins at Dover Beach and runs westwards along a 1.5 km stretch of coast road that runs parallel to Highway 7 as far as Worthing. The beach below the 'gap', or road, is quite rocky and there's not much sand, but there's a wooden boardwalk with benches and the sea here is mostly calm and shallow at low tide and is good for a paddle. St Lawrence Gap is the main nightlife strip on Barbados with many restaurants, bars and clubs, some of which are in idyllic locations overlooking the water. The larger resorts are at the eastern end of Dover Beach (including the two adjacent Sandals resorts that stretch east to Maxwell Beach), while the bars and restaurants, souvenir shops, fast-food outlets and apartment blocks are mostly towards the western end of The Gap. Near the **Southern Palms Hotel**, there's another **Chattel House Village** (the other is at Holetown, page 47), which has several small souvenir and gift shops and a couple of cafés in replicas of traditional brightly painted wooden chattel houses. Dover Beach and The Gap are unashamedly touristy, but the atmosphere is always lively with everybody in a holiday mood.

Perched on a small cliff at the first corner you come to as you enter The Gap from Worthing is **St Lawrence Anglican Church** ① *T420 7679, daily 0900-1700*, which dates from 1838 and is the oldest, most traditional building located along The Gap and is particularly photogenic with the turquoise ocean behind.

Worthing Beach

Just after the church, St Lawrence Gap's lively street turns northwards and joins Highway 7 at Worthing and the string of resorts, apartments, bars and restaurants continues further along the coast past Worthing Beach, also known (rather unimaginatively) as Sandy Beach. The curve of the coastline and an offshore reef has produced a lovely beach with pure white sand and clear, calm, shallow water, almost in a lagoon, making it ideal for families with small children; you may even see turtles. Beach vendors rent out sun loungers, umbrellas and watersports equipment, and there are toilets and showers. At the southeastern end of the beach there are two beach bars worth seeking out for an enjoyable afternoon, both perfectly positioned for sunset-watching. **Crystal Waters Beach Bar** ⓘ *T435 6532, daily 1100-2200*, serves great bar snacks including ham cutters and fishcakes, as well as more substantial meals like blackened fish and macaroni pie, and on Sunday there's a very popular barbecue (phone ahead to make a reservation); food is served 1230-1430 and then there's live music and a party until 1900. Close by is **Carib Beach Bar** ⓘ *T571 4694, www.caribbeachbar.com, daily 1100-2230, last food orders 2130*, which offers a similar Caribbean menu, a live band on Friday evenings from 2000 and a DJ on Sunday from sunset until late. It's a delightful little spot just to relax with a beer; or if you're hungry, the ribs and fishcakes are particularly recommended.

Rockley (Accra) Beach

The next beach west along Highway 7, Rockley Beach is a family-friendly, 300 m curl of white sand. It is often referred to as Accra Beach after the **Accra Beach Hotel & Spa** that dominates it (page 83). Again, it's quite lovely but in the middle of the hotel strip so it is understandably popular and often crowded. There are lifeguards, toilets and showers, and sun loungers and umbrellas can be hired. The many buses that ply the main south coast route stop close to the beach. Behind the sand, wooden stalls sell food and drink and Barbadian crafts in the shade of casuarina and sea grape trees. The southeastern end of the beach is perfect for smaller children as there is a pool-like area protected by rocks that break the force of the waves and where the water stays shallow for a long way out. At the northwestern end, watersports vendors rent out boogie boards, Hobie Cats and windsurfers on the rougher waves. Strong swimmers can head out to a 100 m-long manmade reef of huge boulders for some snorkelling. The reef was sunk in the late 1990s and is now home to coral and large schools of blue tang, jacks and other colourful fish; there's a possibility of seeing hawksbill turtles. It's marked at each end by two large posts protruding from the water and is surrounded by a sandy seabed, but as the waves can break on top of the rock dump, visibility can be poor at times. You must be careful on such a young reef not to damage anything by standing on it or poking around with your hands; coral dies if you touch it.

One of the standout beach bars at Rockley (Accra) Beach is **The Tiki Bar** ⓘ *T435 8074, www.tikibarbados.com, daily 1000-2200*, which has a broad wooden deck at the southeastern end of the beach and offers a good menu, more than 60 cocktails, free sun loungers and showers for patrons, as well as live music on Friday and Saturday evenings. Behind the beach and across Highway 7, the **Quayside Centre** is a small strip mall with beachwear, souvenir and gift shops, a well-stocked supermarket, and a few places to eat including an ice cream parlour and a coffee shop. Just north of the Quayside Centre Shopping Plaza (and not surprisingly on Golf Club Road) is the **Rockley Golf & Country Club** (page 94).

Hastings

The wide, wooden South Coast Boardwalk (officially renamed the Sir Richard Haynes Boardwalk in 2012 after the late Barbadian politician) starts at Rockley (Accra) Beach's western end and zigzags along the shore to just west of the SoCo Hotel in Hastings; almost 1.5 km. It makes a pleasant stroll or a good early morning jog, and a few tiny sandy coves allow you to step down on to the sand for sunbathing or a paddle, although you might need to watch out for crabs. There are a number of bars and restaurants along the route and places to sit and watch the world go by. Police patrol the boardwalk at night, but take care if walking as it is mostly unlit.

Hastings village dates from 1836 and was one of Barbados' first tourist resorts when residents of Bridgetown came by carriage to visit the Hastings Rocks to enjoy the fresh sea breeze. Along the seafront were wooden bathhouses standing in the shallow waters on stilts; bathers would get changed and then descend the stairs into the ocean to swim. Hotels were established in the Hastings area as early as 1887. Today it's practically a suburb of Bridgetown, and where the boardwalk ends, you are on Hastings Main Road (part of Highway 7), which then runs only another kilometre or so westwards to the Garrison Savannah and St Ann's Fort. Hastings has a beautiful white sandy beach dotted with palm trees where turtles are routinely spotted in its crystal-clear waters. With a gently sloping sea shelf, it's safe for children to paddle in – just avoid the rocky sections of the beach; moderate waves and undertow means caution is advised when swimming far out. There are no sun loungers or umbrellas to hire, but plenty of cafés and fast-food outlets can be found just above the beach on Hastings Main Road or back on the boardwalk. Additionally, **Lanterns at Hastings** ⓘ *Hastings Main Rd, Christ Church, T271 0069, see Facebook, daily 0900-2100*, is a modern two-storey mall with 30 shops and restaurants and a large car park.

An unusual attraction in Hastings is the **Mallalieu Motor Collection** ⓘ *Pavilion Court, Hastings Main Rd (Highway 7), T426 4640, www.mallalieu.com/motor-museum, US$10, Mon-Fri 0800-1100, Sat-Sun by appointment.* It is one man's lifetime collection of more than 20 vintage cars crammed into a large garage. The number one vehicle in Bill Mallalieu's line-up is a Bentley made for Prince Bernhard of the Netherlands in 1947 and raced in the 1949 Monte Carlo Rally. There's also a Daimler, Humber, Vanden Plas Princess, Wolseley and Lanchester, among others. Each car has a story to tell and Bill is a great raconteur; he is usually there in the mornings. The walls of the garage are also covered with photographs – the island's first bus, police car, taxi, etc, with pieces of information pinned up alongside. It's an interesting way to spend an hour or so if you like old cars, especially British ones.

Listings Barbados

Tourist information

Barbados National Trust
Wildey House, Wildey, St Michael, T426 2421, www.barbadosnationaltrust.com, see also Facebook. Mon-Fri 0800-1600.
The Barbados National Trust was founded in 1960 and the headquarters is Wildey House, a beautiful Georgian mansion built circa 1760 and set in 2 ha (5 acres) of grounds and woods. It was bequeathed to the Trust by Edna Leacock, and if you visit, ask for a tour (donations appreciated) of the main public rooms to see fine collections of Victorian china, crystal, books and mahogany furniture. The Trust can give you details/schedules for the **Open House Programme** (see box, page 18) and the Sun hikes they organize with the Barbados Hiking Association (page 94).

Barbados Tourism Marketing Inc (BTMI)
One Barbados Place, off ABC Highway near Massy Stores SuperCentre supermarket, Warrens, St Michael, T535 3700, www.visitbarbados.org. Mon-Fri 0830-1630.
BTMI is the tourism authority and promotes Barbados as a tourist destination. The main office is a little way out of the centre of Bridgetown, but nevertheless is very helpful if you drop by and the website is a good source of information. There is also an office at the **Bridgetown Cruise Terminal** (*T426 1718, daily 0900-1700 when cruise ships are in port*). They also maintain offices in New York, Miami, Canada, the UK, Germany and Belgium (see website for contacts). *Ins and Outs of Barbados* (www.insandoutsbarbados.com) is a glossy annual publication with listings from accommodation to car rental and a useful year-round calendar. It's free and can be picked up at larger hotels, and the online version is just as comprehensive. Good free maps published by the tourism associations can also be found at reception desks of hotels and car-hire companies will provide them.

Where to stay

The rates indicated are for the high winter season (Dec-Apr), but remember that, out of season, rates can drop by 30-50%. Hotel VAT (10%) and service charge (10%) is usually a single charge of 20%. Additionally, room rate levy (up to US$13 per night depending on the rate and accommodation class) must be paid locally and directly to the hotel. Be sure to check if these costs have or have not been included in final accommodation quotes. Unless otherwise stated, all hotel rooms have a/c, TV and Wi-Fi.

Bridgetown *maps pages 28-9 and 38.*
The closest accommodation to central Bridgetown is off Bay St to the south, on or near the beaches along Carlisle Bay. Only 1 km or so beyond or east of the Garrison Historic Area on Highway 7 you're in Hastings, the start of a long line of resorts and apartments that goes all the way along the south coast.

$$$ Hilton Barbados Resort
Needhams Point, Aquatic Gap, off Bay St, Bridgetown, St Michael, T426 0200, www.hilton.com/en/hotels/bgihihh-hilton-barbados-resort.
Located between 2 beaches at Needhams Point, the original hotel was opened by Conrad Hilton on the eve of Barbados' independence in 1966, and was replaced in 2005 with this 4-star 350-room double-tower resort. A solid option with excellent service, facilities include multilevel pools, tennis courts, spa, several restaurants and bars. Rates are room-only, B&B or packages with credits to be redeemed at outlets (worth considering as meals and drinks are quite expensive).

$$$ Radisson Aquatica Resort Barbados
Aquatic Gap, off Bay St, Bridgetown, St Michael, T426 4000, www.radissonhotels.com.
Right on Pebbles Beach (you can walk from here to central Bridgetown on the sand), the 4-star Radisson's 124 rooms in a 6-storey block have recently been renovated and those facing Carlisle Bay have terrific views from balconies, especially at sunset. Restaurant, 2 bars, gym and decent-sized pool. Rates are room-only.

$$$ Sweetfield Manor Boutique Hotel
Brittons New Rd, Brittons Hill, Bridgetown, St Michael, T429 8356, www.sweetfield manor.com.
Occupying an early 1900s white-painted, shuttered wooden plantation home on a hilltop in the eastern suburbs of Bridgetown, this atmospheric, upmarket, antique-filled B&B has 10 rooms in the main house or converted outbuildings and stables. Also boasts swimming pool and spa, and the excellent breakfasts run to several courses; the courtyard restaurant **Pavão** – meaning 'Peacock' in Portuguese and referring to the beautiful birds in the gardens – is open to all (page 85).

$$ Nautilus Ocean Suites
Bay St, Bridgetown, St Michael, T426 3541, https://nautilusoceansuites.com.
Nothing fancy but these 15 no-frills apartments in a blue-and-white block are opposite Pebbles Beach and a 15-min walk to central Bridgetown. Dated furnishings but clean with tiled floors and kitchenettes, and some have sofa beds, patios or balconies.

West coast *map page 48.*
The Platinum Coast is so named for its very expensive accommodation, but good-quality cheaper self-catering options can also be found if you are prepared to walk a few mins to the beach.

$$$$ Cobblers Cove
Road View, 1 km south of Speightstown, St Peter, T422 2291, www.cobblerscove.com.
Based around the Great House built in 1943 as a seaside mansion by a plantation owner, this has 40 ultra-chic suites in beautiful bird-filled gardens. The beach is narrow but there's a pool, plus elegant sea-view restaurant (with dress code), spa, watersports, tennis courts and gym. A member of **Relais & Chateaux** with excellent service and a high proportion of repeat well-heeled British clientele. B&B.

$$$$ Colleton Great House
Hwy 1B, Colleton, St Peter, T439 7357, www. colletongreathouse.com.
Dating back to 1652, the 3 ha Colleton Estate features a grand 5-bedroom plantation-style house with swimming pool, a 2-bedroom cottage and 2 apartments, all set amid attractive private gardens and mahogany forest. The house was originally built by an English sugar baron and is now filled with beautiful artwork, Persian rugs, elegant furniture and antique glassware. There are beaches, bars and restaurants within walking distance.

$$$$ Colony Club by Elegant Hotels
Folkestone, St James, T422 2335, www. marriott.com/hotels/travel/bgilc-colony-club-by-elegant-hotels.
A 10-min walk to Holetown, this family-friendly faux-colonial-style low-rise property is popular with British holidaymakers and spreads over mature grounds with soaring palms, mahogany trees and 4 swimming pools. 96 smart rooms with terraces/balconies, large open-air restaurant, swim-up pool bar, and free water taxi to/from other Elegant Hotels on the west coast. Rates are B&B and include non-motorized watersports.

$$$$ Coral Reef Club
Porters, 1.6 km north of Holetown, St James, T422 2372, www.coralreefbarbados.com.
Run by the O'Hara family since the 1950s and spread over 5 ha (12 acres) of glorious gardens with paths, ponds and lawns running down to the sea, this delivers graceful, old-school luxury in 88 plantation-

ON THE ROAD

All-inclusive options on Barbados

The all-inclusive resorts on Barbados sit on beautiful beaches and have one or more swimming pools and watersports. Most packages provide three meals a day, an afternoon snack, appetizers at cocktail hour, and non-alcoholic and house drinks. Breakfast and lunch are normally buffets, while the evening meal might be a themed buffet, a barbecue, or a set menu with three or four choices; the larger resorts can have several restaurants and bars. They vary in price considerably; at the cheaper end they might be sprawling properties featuring blocky-style rooms and mediocre meals, while at the top end are intimate luxury hideaways with stylish interiors and gourmet food. The downsides of staying at an all-inclusive are: unless you eat and drink a lot, their value is not always any greater than paying for meals as you go; some of them can be rather soulless places where you will only mix with guests of one nationality (depending on where the resort is marketed), many of whom may not even leave the property for their entire holiday; the food may start to look and taste similar after a few days; and any extras (boat trips, spa treatments and the like) tend to be expensive. But on the plus side, you know exactly what you are getting for your money (especially if you combine flights and transfers in a package) and service, facilities and location are generally very good. If all-inclusive does appeal, here are some to consider:

The Abidah By Accra, Enterprise (Miami) Beach, Christ Church, www.theabidahhotel.com.
Barbados Beach Club, Maxwell Beach, Christ Church, www.barbadosbeachclub.com.
The Club Barbados Resort & Spa, Holetown, St James, www.theclubbarbados.com.
Coconut Court Beach Hotel, Christ Church, www.coconut-court.com.
Crystal Cove by Elegant Hotels, Appleby, St James, www.marriott.com.
Fairmont Royal Pavilion, Holetown, St James, www.fairmont.com.
Mango Bay Barbados, Holetown, St James, www.mangobaybarbados.com.
Sandals Barbados and **Sandals Royal Barbados**, Dover Beach and Maxwell Beach, Christ Church, www.sandals.com.
Savannah Beach Hotel, Hastings, Christ Church, www.savannahbarbados.com.
Sea Breeze Beach House, Maxwell Beach, Christ Church, www.sea-breeze.com.
SoCo Hotel, Hastings, Christ Church, www.thesocohotel.com.
Sugar Bay Barbados, Hastings, Christ Church, www.sugarbaybarbados.com.
Tamarind by Elegant Hotels, Paynes Bay, St James, www.marriott.com.
Turtle Beach by Elegant Hotels, Dover Beach, Christ Church, www.marriott.com.
Waves Hotel & Spa by Elegant Hotels, Prospect Bay, St James, www.marriott.com.
Wyndham Grand Barbados Sam Lord's Castle, Long Bay, www.wyndhamgrandbarbados.com.

style cottages and villas with wooden balustrading, fretwork and shuttered windows. Elegant dining with evening entertainment, complimentary tennis coaching, spa, and large pool with columns and terrace. B&B, includes non-motorized watersports.

$$$$ The House by Elegant Hotels
Paynes Bay, St James, T432 5525, www.marriott.com.
An adults-only property with 34 modern stylish suites and well regarded for its service and atmosphere – the 'romance concierges' tend to your every need from a jet-lag revival massage to a BBQ on the beach for 2. All-day dining at the restaurant, indulgent champagne breakfasts, 24-hour cocktail bar, sophisticated afternoon tea and evening canapés, and a dine-around option where guests can go to other Elegant Hotel restaurants via water taxi.

$$$$ Little Good Harbour
Shermans, 3 km north of Speightstown, St Lucy, T439 3000, www.littlegoodharbourbarbados.com.
Low-key, relaxed and out of the way, offering 19 attractive wooden cottages with kitchens, some are double-storey with 2-3 bedrooms, set in pretty gardens around 2 pools across the road from the sea, with spa, gym and free kayaks. Room-only or B&B; **The Fish Pot** restaurant is excellent (page 86) and is on the ocean side of the coastal road. Sister hotel to the east-coast **Atlantis Historic Inn** (page 82).

$$$$ Lone Star
Mount Standfast, 3 km north of Holetown, St James, T539 0600, www.thelonestar.com.
Boutique hotel with just 6 huge suites and a private villa with beachfront terraces, stylishly decorated with 4-poster beds and billowing white fabrics. The building was originally a garage built in the 1940s by Romy Reid who ran a bus company and called himself the Lone Star of the west coast; later it was a nightclub and then a house, owned by Mrs Robertson of the jam company who waterskied offshore until her late 80s. The highly regarded restaurant sits right on the beach (page 86). B&B.

$$$$ The Sandpiper
Holetown, St James, T422 2251, www.sandpiperbarbados.com.
More informal than the sister property **Coral Reef Club** (page 79), but still luxurious and spread around tropical gardens, 50 rooms and suites, some with kitchenette, 2 swimming pools, a romantic open-air restaurant fringed by koi-filled ponds, inviting beach bar, gym and 2 tennis courts. Guests can use the spa and restaurant at Coral Reef Club, a 10-min drive away (free transfers are provided). B&B.

$$$ Bayfield House
Crescent Dr, Mullins, St Peter, T419 0497, www.bayfieldbarbados.com.
Impeccably run, this 1930s plantation-style guesthouse is up a quiet side lane about a 5-min walk to Mullins Beach. It sits in an expansive garden with a cannon on the front lawn and an attractive oval swimming pool. The 10 rooms share the large wrap-around verandas furnished with rocking chairs and fern-filled pots. B&B and dinners are offered a couple of nights a week. No TVs or children under 12.

$$$ Beach View Barbados
Paynes Bay, St James, T432 2300, www.beachviewbarbados.com.
On the inland side of the coastal road and a 2-min walk to Paynes Bay beach, these 36 1- to 3-bedroom apartments and 10 2-storey villas (all with dishwasher, washing machine and dryer) are popular with families and are arranged in a U-shape around a pool area with neat lawns and floral walkways. Room-only, but all meals provided by the on-site **Sugar Café**.

$$$ Legend Garden Condos
Highway 1B, Mullins, St Peter, T422 8369, see Facebook.
Up an extended driveway opposite Mullins Beach, these 9 1- and 2-bed spacious and good-value apartments have well-equipped kitchens and futons or sofa beds, and are set in quiet tropical gardens with a pool, patios,

barbecues, and the odd green monkey. Rates are room-only but restaurants and bus stop close by.

$$$ Sugar Cane Club Hotel & Spa
Maynards, St Peter, T422 5026, www.sugarcaneclub.com.
An inland 4-star option set in peaceful grounds with tiered lawns where you can often see green monkeys. The 56 spacious rooms in Mediterranean-style whitewashed and terracotta-roofed buildings have kitchenettes and patios/balconies. Facilities include 2 pools, spa, gym, mountain bikes, 2 restaurants and bars. Free daytime shuttles to Heywoods Beach (2 km) and Speightstown (3 km). Room-only or all-inclusive, no children under 14.

$$$ Tropical Sunset Beach Apartment Hotel
West Haven Complex, Holetown, St James, T432 2715, www.tropicalsunsetbarbados.com.
This 4-storey modern block is one of the cheapest places on the west coast and it's right on Holetown's beach. 23 simple but adequate apartments with kitchenettes and balcony, can sleep a family of 4, small pool and sun loungers on the beach, lots of restaurants close by and a Massy Stores supermarket across the road.

East coast *map pages 48-9.*

$$$ The Atlantis Historic Inn
Tent Bay, Bathsheba, St Joseph, T433 9445, www.atlantishotelbarbados.com.
A 10-min walk to Bathsheba Beach, in a spectacular setting with waves crashing below, this hotel opened in 1884 alongside the railway line and became a much-loved institution under the management of Enid Maxwell who ran it 1945-2001. Now owned by the Kirby and Warden families, who also own **Little Good Harbour** on the west coast, it has 8 rooms and 2 apartments, and is elegant and understated with whitewashed tongue-and-groove panelling, louvred shutters and muslin-swathed beds. B&B, good restaurant, popular with day trippers, especially for the Sun buffet lunch (page 87).

$$$ ECO Lifestyle & Lodge
Tent Bay, Bathsheba, St Joseph, T433 9450, www.ecolifestylelodge.com.
Relaxing and peaceful guesthouse with rustic charm, a 10-min walk to Bathsheba Beach, 10 rooms in 2 wooden houses with whitewashed walls and shutters, most have kitchenettes, and hammocks on the balconies and between palm trees on the lawns. Eco practices include solar-heated power and using recycled products, and the restaurant menu features locally grown organic produce (fish available but no meat). There's no pool, but jacuzzi and sauna, and on Tue & Thu complimentary transport to/from west coast beaches. Room-only, no children under 12.

$$ Round House
Bathsheba, St Joseph, T433 9678, www.roundhousebarbados.com.
Built in 1832 as a private house and perched above Bathsheba Beach overlooking the famous Soup Bowl, this quirky B&B has 5 rooms in the domed rounded section (hence the name); each different, from a tiny single to a large double with roof terrace, but all light and bright, and original skylights and staircases provide unique charm. The excellent restaurant is Bathsheba's best place to eat in the evenings (page 87).

South coast *map pages 48-9.*
Most of the south coast is wall-to-wall hotels from Hastings to Dover popular with package holidaymakers. It's close to the airport, with plenty of watersports and nightlife.

$$$$ The Crane
Crane, St Philip, T423 6220, www.thecrane.com.
The original Crane Hotel first opened in 1887 as a retreat for plantation owners and sits in a spectacular clifftop setting.

Today it's a vast but attractively designed gated resort and timeshare complex with 252 spacious and modern rooms and apartments with patios/balconies, and some with private plunge pools. Top-notch facilities include a glass elevator down to the pink-sand Crane Beach, 5 swimming pools, including an impressive 6000 sq m (1½ acre) cascading complex, 2 floodlit tennis courts, 6 restaurants and bars, spa, gym and the Crane Village shopping mall. Rates are room-only.

$$$$ Little Arches Boutique Hotel
Enterprise Beach Rd, Christ Church, T420 4689, www.littlearches.com.
This super-friendly, vibrant salmon-pink, hacienda-style adults-only hotel is 150 m from Enterprise (Miami) Beach and has quirky colourful touches such as mosaic tiles, chandeliers and a triangular-shaped swimming pool. The excellent restaurant, **Café Luna** (page 87) is on the rooftop with sea views. The 10 rooms all have terracotta floors, 4-poster beds and attractive bathrooms but vary in size and price – the cheapest don't have private terraces, while the more expensive have plunge pools. Rates are room-only.

$$$$ O$_2$ Beach Club & Spa
Dover Rd, Christ Church, T418 1800, www.o2beachclubbarbados.com.
Good location on Dover Beach and the Gap, this super-chic and upscale all-inclusive opened in 2021 and has 130 rooms, suites and apartments in three different 'collections' (Club, Luxury and Concierge), on 7 floors with balconies, all with stylish décor and extras like bottle of champagne and turn-down service. Nice snake-shaped pool with swim-up bar and another pool on the rooftop, 5 dining 'concepts', 7 bars, and spa with the only hammam on Barbados.

$$$$-$$$ Southern Palms Beach Club
St Lawrence Gap, Christ Church, T428 7171, www.southernpalms.net.
In a great location right on Dover Beach, this smart but unpretentious pink-and-white resort has 92 rooms with balconies/patios and Caribbean-style décor; suites have kitchenettes and pull-out sofas for children. Very popular with British guests, 2 pools, gym, and lively beachside restaurant/bar: **Garden Terrace** (*open to all, 0730-2200*). B&B includes afternoon tea and non-motorized watersports.

$$$ Accra Beach Hotel & Spa
Rockley (Accra) Beach, Christ Church, T435 8920, www.accrabeachhotel.com.
Popular 4-star option with prime beach access (Rockley Beach is known as Accra Beach because of the hotel), plus a large family pool and another adults-only one with swim-up bar, gym and spa, kids' club, and 3 restaurants offering regular themed buffets and live entertainment. 221 comfortable rooms, most with sofa beds and balconies; pay more for ocean views. Room-only or meal plans available.

$$$ Bougainvillea Barbados
Maxwell Coast Rd, Christ Church, T628 0990, www.bougainvillearesort.com.
Right on Maxwell Beach, this family-friendly resort has 100 bright rooms in several cream and pink 4-storey blocks, all with kitchens and some sleep 4. Facilities include 3 swimming pools, spa, kids' club, free use of boogie boards, kayaks and snorkelling gear, and both the casual **Calabash Café** and **Deia Restaurant** have attractive beachfront wooden decks and are open to all. Room-only or meal plans available.

$$$ Coral Sands Beach Resort
Worthing Beach, T435 6617, www.coralsandsresort.com.
Affordable 3-star family resort right on Worthing Beach and away from the main road (Highway 7), with 31 large sea-view studios with 2 double beds, kitchenettes, extra-large balconies, floral décor and white wicker furniture. There's a decent bar by the smallish pool but the dining room is characterless; rates are room-only so better to self-cater (a good

supermarket is nearby) and it's only a 5-min walk to restaurants at The Gap.

$$$ Magic Isle Beach Apartments
Rockley Beach, Christ Church, T435 6760, www.magicislebarbados.com.
Simple and slightly old-fashioned but clean and well maintained, 30 sea-facing 1- and 2-bed apartments, a gate at the bottom of the garden dotted with a few palms and a good-sized pool leads directly on to one end of Rockley (Accra) Beach and the boardwalk, and there's a supermarket and a number of affordable places to eat and drink close by.

$$$ The Rockley by Ocean Hotels
Rockley Main Rd (Highway 7), Rockley, Christ Church, T435 8561, www.therockleybarbados.com.
Formerly known as South Beach Hotel, a smart white block with glass balconies next to Quayside Centre mall and across the road from Rockley (Accra) Beach and the boardwalk. 49 1- and 2-bed studios in contemporary Bajan-inspired décor, with sofa beds, well-equipped kitchens (pre-arrival grocery shopping can be arranged), large pool with bar, restaurant for buffet breakfasts and plenty of affordable places to eat nearby. B&B.

$$$ Yellow Bird Hotel
St Lawrence Gap, Christ Church, T622 8444, www.yellowbirdbarbados.com.
Across the street from the narrow beach at St Lawrence Bay, a 2-min walk to better Worthing Beach and right at the start of The Gap at the western end, this personable family-run hotel has 22 rooms and apartments, all with cheerful décor and Bajan artwork, sofa beds and sea-facing balconies. There's a pool, and the affordable **On the Bay** restaurant (*open to all, 0730-2030*), is good for a leisurely breakfast overlooking the bay and boardwalk. Room-only or B&B.

$$$-$$ Butterfly Beach Hotel
Maxwell Main Rd (Highway 7), Oistins, Christ Church, T428 9095, www.butterflybeach.com.
Low-key and good-value beachfront hotel with 92 modern and bright units with either floor-to-ceiling windows or balconies; rooms have fridge and kettle, and apartments neat kitchenettes. There's only a strip of narrow sand here but it has 2 pools with sun decks and whirlpools, plus the **Reef Bar and Grill**; there's a bus stop outside and **Oistins Fish Fry** (see box, page 74) is within walking distance. Room-only or meal plans available.

$$ Manderley Villas
Mangrove, St Philip, T234 5778.
Located in a quiet village a short distance inland, this small place is run by a warm and welcoming couple, offering clean and spacious modern apartments with kitchenette and laundry facilities. It's just 3 km from the airport, 2 km from Foul Bay Beach, and 10 mins' walk from a market. It would be ideal for those with a rental car looking for a modestly priced base, but airport pick-up is available for those without a car.

$$ OceanBlue Resort
Inch Marlow, Christ Church, T262 0919, www.oceanblue-resort.com.
Formerly known as Peach & Quiet, the attractive complex features an apartment and 22 modern rooms, many with an ocean view. Note that there is no beach directly in front of the hotel, but Silver Rock Beach and Long Beach are within 10 mins' walk. There is a smart swimming pool featuring a swim-up bar, and a good restaurant on site (open to outside guests by reservation only). No hotel guests under 16.

$$ Time Out Hotel
St Lawrence Gap, Dover, Christ Church, T420 5021, www.timeoutbarbados.com.
Opposite Dover Beach at the eastern end of The Gap, this budget hotel is a favourite with beach-goers and night owls alike. The 76 rooms are a bit plain, but are spotless with kettle and mini-fridge; most have balconies/patios, although the roadside ones can be noisy. Pool with shady palms and **Rhum Stop** is the lively restaurant/bar (*open to all, 0730-*

late) with karaoke Wed, live music Thu-Sat, and brunch on Sun. B&B with continental breakfast (pay extra for cooked items).

$$-$ Ocean Spray Apartments
Surfer's Point, Inch Marlow, Christ Church, T428 5426, www.oceansprayapartments.com.

A bit off the beaten track for the south coast in Inch Marlow and a 5-min bus ride to the nearest swimming beach, but super-peaceful and right on Surfer's Point with wind- and kitesurfing at nearby Silver Rock and Long Beach. 25 simple and good-value studio, 1- and multiple-room apartments with ocean views and well-equipped kitchenettes. Yoga can be organized, as well as hiking at **Coco Hills Forest** (page 51).

Restaurants

In the peak winter months, make reservations at the smart restaurants a long way in advance, especially for a waterfront or sunset-facing table. The 17.5% VAT and a 2.5% product levy are included in menu prices, but most restaurants also automatically add a 10% service charge to the bill, and sometimes 15% for tables of 10 or more – beware of tipping twice.

Bridgetown *maps pages 28-9 and 38.*

$$$ Lobster Alive
Bay St, Brownes Beach, T435 0305, www.lobsteralive.net. Mon-Sat 1200-2100, Sun 1200-1700.

Famous for its lobster which you choose from the tank and have cooked fresh to order (it's very expensive and flown in from the Grenadines). But other local seafood includes crab backs, conch and chowder. An open relaxed venue on Brownes Beach with sun loungers and umbrellas during the day and great live jazz at Sun lunch.

$$$ Pavão
Sweetfield Manor Boutique Hotel, T429 8356, https://sweetfieldmanor.com. daily 0630-1030 & 1200-1500, Wed-Sun 1700-2200.

Located in a lovely courtyard at Sweetfield Manor (page 79), this highly rated fine-dining restaurant fuses European, Asian and Caribbean cuisines; expect the likes of duck, lamb, pork, lobster and local fish, as well as decadently rich desserts. Sushi night is on Wed, on Sat there's a generous brunch, and the cocktail list is impressive.

$$$-$$ Sage Bistro
Upper Bay Street, Bridgetown, St Michael, T228 7243, www.sagebarbados.com. Tue-Sun 0800-1600.

This cosy little gem offers a vibrant menu of Bajan fare with a creative twist (their flying fish sandwiches come in for particular praise), as well as a good selection of light bites such as chicken wraps or calamari. Breakfast here is especially recommended, catering to all tastes whether you prefer pancakes, avocado toast, granola, omelette, or a hearty platter of eggs, bacon, sausage and beans.

$ Balcony
1st floor, Bridgetown Duty Free Department Store, Broad St, T539 4686. Mon-Fri 1100-1530.

Go early because this is popular with locals and the queue gets long for the buffet lunches. Choose a small or large plate, pile it with salads, macaroni pie and all the trimmings, then pay for your portion of meat or fish and wash it down with a Banks beer. Great place to eat local food at local prices and a good spot for people-watching on Broad St below.

$ Cuz's Fish Stand
Aquatic Gap, off Bay St, T254 8928. Sun-Fri 1130-1730.

The fish cutter sandwich is a Bajan obsession, and this legendary decades-old blue-and-yellow clapboard hut on Pebbles Beach is a great place to try one; fried marlin or flying fish in a bread roll with salad from around US$7, and a little more with cheese and egg, hot sauce and other dressings. Popular and there's usually a queue at lunchtime. No frills, cash only.

$ Mustors Harbour
McGregor St, T426 5175, see Facebook. Mon-Fri 1030-1500.

This family business has been in operation since 1941 and has a snackette downstairs for substantial breakfasts, Bajan fishcakes, flying fish cutters and other hot snacks, while a more formal restaurant is upstairs for tasty, filling Bajan food like fried or stew chicken with rice and peas, pork chops with macaroni pie or cou-cou and salad.

West coast *map page 48.*

$$$ Cariba
Clarke's Gap, Derricks, T432 8737, www.caribarestaurant.com. Nov-Apr daily, May-Oct Mon-Sat, 1800-2130.

Run by a friendly hands-on chef who once worked at Sandy Lane, this informal (for the west coast) dinner option offers tasty Asian, Caribbean and seafood dishes; try the shrimp curry or steak in rum sauce and save room for the signature Bajan bread-and-butter pudding with cinnamon ice cream.

$$$ Fusion Rooftop
Holetown, St James, T271 1258, www.fusionrooftop.com. Mon-Sat 1730-2300.

Pricey high-end venue, with sleek and contemporary décor and wonderful views; tables are under the retractable roof of the Limegrove Lifestyle Centre, which is pulled back to reveal the stars. Delicately plated food from lobster to lamb, a separate sushi menu, delicious desserts and, in high season, live music on Mon and Wed and a DJ on Fri.

$$$ Lone Star
See Where to stay, page 81. Breakfast daily 0830-1000, lunch Thu-Mon 1100-1430, dinner Mon-Sun 1730-2300.

This super-chic upmarket restaurant is a favourite on the Platinum Coast and has a large deck spreading on to the sand with overhead fans, giant mirrors, artwork, stylish blue-and-white décor and a sophisticated cocktail lounge. The menu is a fusion of European, Asian and Caribbean dishes, with steaks, lamb and duck plus local seafood; the lunchtime menu offers lighter meals such as catch of the day or wood-fired pizza.

$$$ The Tides
Balmore House, Holetown, St James, T432 8356, www.tidesbarbados.com. Breakfast Fri-Sun 0800-1030, lunch Tue-Sun 1200-1400, dinner daily 1700-2200.

This waterfront restaurant offers a fine dining menu of seafood with Asian touches, meat and vegetarian dishes, decadent desserts, all served on a magical terrace with a boardwalk between the tables and the sea, and trees growing through the roof of the building. Live music several nights a week. Arrive early for drinks at the bar which doubles up as an art gallery.

$$$-$$ The Fish Pot
At Little Good Harbour, see Where to stay, page 81, T439 3000, www.fishpotbarbados.com. Daily by reservation only, 0800-1030 & 1200-2030.

Located in 18th-century Fort Rupert directly on the water's edge with coral stone walls, an open-air terrace and imaginative menu. Standout items include octopus salad, pan-fried mahi mahi and herb-crusted tuna, and lighter lunches include pastas, panini and stir-fries. After breakfast/lunch you can swim, and at dinner book a table overlooking the ocean for an amazing sunset view.

$$$-$$ The Mews
2nd St, Holetown, T432 1122, www.themewsbarbados.com. Mon-Sat 1830-2130, bar 1700-late, opens Sun Sep and Dec-Jan.

Quite expensive but superb food with a mix of local and European dishes focusing on 'farm-to-table' seasonal menus served in a very pretty house with contemporary art on the walls, tables upstairs on the balcony or interior patio, and lively bar with a tapas menu downstairs.

$$ The Sea Shed
Highway 1B, Mullins, just south of Speightstown, St Peter, T572 5111,

www.seashedbarbados.com. Daily, bar open from 1100, food 1100-2100.
Stylish beach bar/restaurant with service to your sun lounger, offering tasty tapas, seafood and steaks, and good vegetarian options. A great spot for sunset-watching; on Sun there is a chilled party with DJ, extended lunch menu until 1600 and pizzas until 1900.

$ Fisherman's Pub
Queen's St, Speightstown, St Peter, T422 2703, see Facebook. Mon-Sat 1100-2230, & Sun Nov-Mar.
A Speightstown institution that opened in 1939 to provide meals to local fishermen and now a deservedly popular lunch stop for tourists on island tours, with tables on a seafront terrace. Good Bajan food includes breadfruit cou-cou, fish head soup with dumplings, flying fish and sweet potato pie, all at very reasonable prices and served buffet-style at busier lunchtimes.

East coast *map pages 48-9.*

$$$-$$ Zemi East Coast Café
Hillcrest, Bathsheba, St Joseph, T571 9172, www.linktr.ee/zemicafe. Wed-Sun 1100-1700.
A beautifully relaxed venue in a stunning seafront location serving a range of meat and fish dishes, salads and sandwiches, as well as good coffee and cocktails. Maybe not the cheapest of eateries but the fishcakes are to die for and their guava cheesecake garners similar acclaim.

$$ The Atlantis Historic Inn
See Where to stay, page 82. Daily (except closed Sun Nov-Apr) 0800-1000 & 1200-1530, dinner by reservation only 1700-1900.
Famous for its Bajan buffet lunches on Sun with live music, which might feature conch (lambi) fritters, jerk pork, curried yam or goat or pepperpot stew, while at other times and at dinner is a sophisticated menu of seafood, duck, beef and good vegetarian options such as chickpea burgers and couscous salads. Great east coast views from the breezy terrace.

$$ Naniki
Surinam, St Joseph, T433 1300, www.nanikibarbados.com. Tue-Sun 1230-1530.
Perched high in the hills of the Scotland District overlooking the coast, Naniki is tricky to find but well worth the effort; turn off Highway 3 just south of St Joseph's church. A Bajan lunch of grilled seafood, poultry or pork served with local favourites like yam, breadfruit and sweet potato is served with a great view over fields and palm trees from the deck; guided hike and country Saturday lime (a traditional casual Bajan get-together) on Sat from 1000, jazz buffet lunch on Sun, and also rents out cottages on the property. *Naniki* is an Arawak word meaning 'spirited' or 'full of life'.

$$ Round House
See Where to stay, page 82. High season Mon-Fri 1100-1600, Sat-Sun 0900-1600; low season closed Mon-Thu (phone ahead).
Lovely location overlooking the pounding surf in Bathsheba with fresh ocean breezes from the terrace, very popular for brunch or lunch on island tours. A long menu of Caribbean and international features everything from fishcakes and club sandwiches to cheeseburgers and catch of the day. There's a good choice of wines and cocktails.

South coast *map pages 48-9.*

$$$ Café Luna
At Little Arches Boutique Hotel, see Where to stay, page 83, T428 6172, www.cafelunabarbados.com. Breakfast Mon-Fri 0900-1100, lunch Mon-Fri 1130-1430, brunch Sat-Sun 0900-1430, dinner daily 1700-2130 (last orders 2100), by reservation only.
Fine dining on the rooftop terracotta terrace of this charming hotel with a superb menu of Caribbean, Asian and Mediterranean dishes created by acclaimed Canadian chef Mark de Gruchy (or Moo as he is better known). Very romantic and atmospheric, ocean views over Enterprise (Miami) Beach, special events

like Bajan and sushi nights, go early for sundowner cocktails from 1700.

$$$ Champers
Skeetes Hill, Christ Church, T434 3463, www.champersrestaurant.com. Lunch Sun-Fri 1130-1400, dinner Mon-Sat 1700-2100.
Overlooking Rockley (Accra) Beach and one of the best restaurants on the south coast, this offers waterfront dining on the terrace or upstairs balcony. Superb food with interesting flavour combinations and culinary styles from Cajun to teriyaki, long list of gooey desserts and excellent service. Reservations essential for a good table.

$$$ Coral Reef Club
See Where to stay, page 79. Daily 1300-1430 & 1930-2130, by reservation only.
Elegant dining in this top-notch, 5-star hotel where the restaurant, on an oceanfront covered terrace, offers a daily changing à la carte menu, mostly French cuisine infused with local Caribbean ingredients. There's live music most nights, a Bajan/international buffet on Mon night, and a barbecue on Thu night followed by a floor show featuring limbo dancing, folk dancing and fire-eating.

$$$-$$ Harlequin
St Lawrence Gap, Christ Church, T420 7677, www.harlequinrestaurant.com. Daily 1800-2200.
One of the most popular restaurants on The Gap thanks to the consistently good food, hands-on service, colourful décor and vibey atmosphere. Long menu featuring seafood, grills, Italian and vegetarian dishes, and house specialities include coconut shrimp, fish chowder and Cajun chicken.

$$ Café Sol
St Lawrence Gap, Christ Church, T420 7655, www.cafesolbarbados.com. Mon 1700-2300, Tue-Sun 1130-2300.
Lively Mexican restaurant at the western end of The Gap famous for its 15 flavours of margaritas (by the glass or jug), with a menu of all the usual Tex-Mex dishes such as nachos, fajitas, tacos and chimichangas. There's often a party mood and 2 happy hours (1700-1900 and 2200-0000).

$$ Naru Restaurant & Lounge
Highway 7, Hastings, Christ Church, T228 6278, www.narubarbados.com. Mon-Sat 1700-2100.
Popular and casual spot on the South Coast Boardwalk with open kitchen, engaging staff and a menu that blends Caribbean and Japanese dishes – there's something for everybody, from pork chops and sweet potato mash to bento boxes and maki rolls. Well-priced and also does take-away.

$$ Tapas
Highway 7, Hastings, Christ Church, T228 0704, www.tapasbarbados.com. Daily 1130-2230, bar until 0000 Sat-Sun.
With a breezy deck alongside the South Coast Boardwalk, this buzzy mid-priced venue has a menu of substantial and varied Caribbean/Asian/Mediterranean tapas such as spicy Thai fishcakes, smoked marlin pâté or shark fritters, as well as more expensive full meals and a long list of cocktails.

$ Bliss Cafe
Dover Rd, Christ Church, T255 5140, see Facebook. Wed-Sun 0800-1430.
Those on room-only hotel rates could head to this cheerful family-run café and bakery at the eastern end of The Gap for a 'blissful' breakfast or filling lunch. It offers a full English and creamy omelettes and the stuffed panini/bagels/flatbreads/pitas and loaded sweet waffles go for US$9-13. Gluten-free, vegan and halal options, good coffees and the delicious fresh juices include sorrel, beetroot and ginger.

$ Just Grillin'
Quayside Centre, Highway 7, Rockley, Christ Church, T435 6469, www.justgrillinbarbados.com. Mon-Sat 1130-2200, Sun 1600-2200.
Open-sided eatery where you place orders at a window, wait to be called, then eat at shared wooden tables. Options include huge portions of steak, ribs, chicken and

fish served with vegetables, salad, rice or potatoes; also sandwiches and serves alcohol. There's a second branch near the Chattel Village shops on Highway 1 in Holetown.

$ Surfers Café
Highway 7, Oistins, Christ Church, T435 5996, see Facebook. Daily 0700-2130.
On the western side of Oistins opposite the Massy Stores supermarket and with a balcony overlooking the bay, this surfer-themed laid-back café/bar has good service and food, with cooked breakfasts, salads, grilled catch of the day from Oistins Fish Market, coffees and cocktails, and stays open late on Fri and Sat.

Bars and clubs

Barbados is lively after dark, and nightlife ranges from no-frills rum shops and sports bars to flashy cocktail bars, nightclubs and dinner shows. On the south coast at St Lawrence Gap are a concentration of bars and clubs in close proximity to each other, while on the west coast are a clutch of rather more salubrious bars on 1st St and 2nd St in the heart of Holetown, but every hotel has a bar and rum shops are found even in the tiniest settlement. The biggest street party on the island is the Oistins Fish Fry; see box, page 74.

Bar 557
Lower Carter's Gap, Bridgetown, Christ Church, T231 5915. Thu-Sun 1700-2200.
A pleasant little bar with indoor and outdoor seating; a chilled place run by the very friendly Donovan. He offers great rum punch, good burgers and outstanding grilled fish – the day's menu being chalked up on a surfboard-shaped blackboard.

Bubba's Sports Bar & Restaurant
Highway 7, Rockley, Christ Church, T435 8731, www.bubbassportsbar.net. Tue-Sun 0800-2200.
A cavernous bar famous for its 3 10 ft screens plus an astonishing 22 other TVs for watching sports – British soccer, NBA basketball, NFL football, Formula One – while you eat and drink. Also offers a Sun buffet breakfast.

Club Rehab
Fontabelle Rd, Bridgetown, St Michael, Instagram @clubrehab_. Daily 2200-0600.
Don't be fooled by its modest exterior: if you're seeking adult entertainment then a wild night with exotic local dancers and plenty of alcohol is the theme of this joint. Check @clubrehab_ on Instagram for upcoming special party nights.

The Cove
St Lawrence Gap, Christ Church, T420 7612. Daily 2000-0300.
Classic large nightclub on The Gap attracting a youthful crowd, locals and holidaymakers, indoor and outdoor dance floors, and a wide range of music, from reggae and calypso to mainstream pop. Cover US$6-13 and happy hour 2100-2300.

Drift Ocean Terrace Lounge
Highway 1, opposite the Chattel Village, Holetown, St James, T233 5404, https://driftloungebarbados.com. Daily 1130-1530, 1700 until late.
Lovely location with tables on a deck overlooking the sea or inside in a/c lounge with giant sofas, artwork on the walls, and chilled music. Excellent cocktails, good wine list, authentic thin-crust pizzas, and savoury and sweet 'night bites' like mini-burgers and chocolate brownies served on platters to share.

Harbour Lights
Bay St, Bridgetown, St Michael, T436 7225, www.harbourlightsbarbados.com. Nightclub Fri 2100-0200, US$35 entry inclusive of drinks; US$117 dinner and show Wed-Thu 1900-2230, reduced prices for under 17s.
An open-air venue on the beach at Carlisle Bay that has 2 dance floors and bars, a grill restaurant and is pumping with music, lively and crowded. The Mon and Wed 'Beach Extravaganza Dinner Show' includes a Bajan barbecue, drinks, and a show featuring fire eaters, stilt walkers, limbo dancers and steel

pan performers. It is suitable for families early on (before the nightclub) and includes hotel transfers.

Little Bristol Beach Bar
Queen's St, Speightstown, St Peter, T439 1592, see Facebook. Wed-Sun 1200-1930.
Speightstown was originally called Little Bristol and this unassuming bar has a deck overlooking the town pier. Not a late-night spot but is west-facing so popular with regulars and visitors for sundowners. Reasonably priced booze, great rum cocktails, snacks like fishcakes and curry rotis from a small food truck, and live music on Wed, Fri and Sun from 1730.

MOJO Bar & The Chopping Board Kitchen
Highway 7, Worthing, Christ Church, T435 9008. Mon-Sat 1000-0200.
Established south coast bar with pictures of musicians decorating the walls and a back room devoted to Bob Marley. Excellent cocktails and good food at the adjoining Chopping Board Kitchen, including gourmet burgers, steaks, fish and pasta at reasonable prices (kitchen closes at 2300 but late-night snacks available).

The Sipping Room
Hastings Main Rd, Christ Church, T547 6293, www.sippingroom246.com. Tue-Fri 1600-2300, Sat-Sun 0900-1300 & 1600-0000.
A chic and intimate New York-style lounge with great ambience, friendly service and regular live entertainment, including music and comedy (check Facebook or Instagram for upcoming acts). The bar serves some of the best cocktails on the island, and a rather decent food menu to boot.

The Tipsy Monkey Sports Bar
1st St, Holetown, St James, T538 4779, www.tipsymonkeybb.com. Mon 1600-2200, Wed-Thu 1000-2200, Fri-Sun 1000-late.
The best place for live sports on the west coast, from footie to F1 and cricket to hockey. Good cold beers and rum punch served in a comfortable and relaxing atmosphere. Menu highlights include BBQ pulled pork sliders, Korean wings, nachos, and ribeye steak.

TML One Love Bar
1st St, Holetown, St James, T432 1444, see Facebook. Daily 0900-2300.
A real Bajan liming spot in a cheery blue-and-yellow chattel-style house on popular 1st St. Great place to pull up a chair and chat, drinks specials like 5 Banks beers on ice for US$14. If you're a fan of karaoke then be sure to visit on a Sunday night from 2000, when the throng of enthusiastic revellers often blocks the whole street!

Wendy's Sports Bar
Risk Rd, off Highway 1, Fitts Village, St James, T571 5512, m.wendyssportsbar.com. Tue-Sat 1000-2200.
Winning combination of 15 screens to watch sport (especially European soccer) and affordable Bajan food like pork ribs, BBQ pigtails, grilled fish and macaroni pie, as well as full English breakfasts. Fun, informal atmosphere, decorated in cricket and football shirts and Banks beer flags.

West Bar
Limegrove Lifestyle Centre, Holetown, St James, T571 7300, www.westbarbarbados.com. Mon-Thu 0800-2300, Fri-Sat 0800-0100.
In the Limegrove's courtyard, a popular west coast bar aimed at both shoppers and after-work liming offering a vast choice of expensive cocktails, wines, cognacs, gins and whiskies. Tasty food includes healthy breakfasts, club sandwiches, Bajan platters and bar bites.

Entertainment

Cinemas
Globe Drive-In, *Adams Castle, not far from Sheraton Mall, off Tom Adams Highway, Christ Church, T437 0479, www.globedrive-in.com. Wed-Sun 1730-2100, US$18, children (under 12) US$10 per movie.* Drive-in with 2 movies back-to-back, and a canteen for take-aways and popcorn.
Olympus Theatres, *Sheraton Mall, Sargeants Village, Christ Church, T228 5255,*

www.olympus.bb. Tue-Sun 1400-2100, US$9, children (under 12) US$6. A 6-screen multiplex with snack bar.

Theatres
Daphne Joseph Hackett Theatre, *Queen's Park House, Queen's Park, Bridgetown, T271 0060, www.ncf.bb.* Upstairs from Queen's Park Gallery, this 200-seat theatre is named after Daphne Joseph Hackett (1915-1988), a Bajan teacher, scriptwriter, actor and director who did much to develop theatre in the Caribbean. Run by the National Cultural Foundation, it hosts occasional performances, films and fashion shows.

Shopping

Barbados has some of the best shopping in the Caribbean and, although prices are high, the range of goods available is excellent. Duty-free shopping for jewellery, cosmetics, perfumes, electronics and designer goods and the like is well advertised with discounts of 30-50% – you need to present your passport, airline ticket or (if on a cruise) travel documents at the point of sale. A duty-free shopping centre for cruise-ship passengers is at the Bridgetown Cruise Terminal and there are duty-free outlets at Grantley Adams International Airport. **Bridgetown Duty Free** (www.bridgetowndutyfree.com) is a duty-free chain of shops with its main store on Broad St in Bridgetown and other outlets in shopping centres. **Broad St** and **Swan St** are the principal shopping areas in the centre of Bridgetown, and there are a number of modern malls around the island.

Art galleries
Barbados Arts Council Gallery, *Pelican Craft Centre, Harbour Rd, Bridgetown, T426 4385, www.thebarbadosartscouncil.com. Mon-Fri 0900-1700, Sat 0900-1300.* A non-profit organization set up to foster Barbadian art from both established artists with an international reputation and those just starting out.

Gallery of Caribbean Art, *Northern Business Centre, Queen's St, Speightstown, St Peter, T419 0858, www.artgallerycaribbean.com. Mon-Fri 1000-1600, Sat 1000-1400.* A range of contemporary art, sculpture and photography from all around the Caribbean.
On The Wall Art Gallery, *at Limegrove Lifestyle Centre (page 92), Holetown, St James, Mon-Sat 1000-1700; and Champers restaurant (page 88), Skeetes Hill, Christ Church, open restaurant hours, Mon-Sun 1130-1400 & 1730-2100, Sat 1700-2100. T234 9145, www.onthewallartgallery.com.* A fine art and craft gallery showcasing local artists of varying styles and mediums.
Queen's Park Gallery, *Queen's Park House, Queen's Park, Bridgetown, T427 2345, www.ncf.bb. Mon-Fri 0900-1600, Sat 0900-1400.* Run by the National Cultural Foundation, it exhibits and sells paintings, sculptures, prints and other work from emerging and established Barbadian artists.

Crafts
Best of Barbados, *Chattel Village, Holetown, T538 6915; Southern Palms Hotel, St Lawrence Gap, T538 6917; Quayside Centre, Rockley, T538 6916; Bridgetown Cruise Terminal, T538 6913; and the departure area of the airport, T538 6911, www.best-of-barbados.com.* The ultimate gift shop with every Barbados souvenir imaginable. The designs mostly stem from the work of Jill Walker, who has been living and painting on Barbados since 1956, and they have a network of cottage workers making things exclusively for the shop. Her prints of local scenes are on sale, as well as mugs, candles and T-shirts.
Earthworks Pottery, *Edgehill Heights No 2, St Thomas, to get here turn off Highway 2A on Padmore Village Rd just north of Warrens, T425 0223, www.earthworkspottery.com. Mon-Fri 0900-1700, Sat 0900-1300.* A large showroom of desirable hand-decorated bowls, pots, jugs and tableware (the coffee pots in the shape of Bajan chattel houses are fun), everything is handmade and you can see the

potters at work, and the Arthouse Café has a pleasant veranda. Next door is the **H P Batik Studio** (*T424 0391*) run by talented artist Henderson Reece, who creates colourful Barbados pictures, plus dresses, scarves, bags and men's shirts, and also runs one-day workshops teaching batik.

Pelican Craft Centre, *Princess Alice Highway, between Bridgetown Cruise Terminal and Princess Alice Bus Terminal, Bridgetown, T622 1683. Mon-Sat 0900-1630.* Good displays of craft items, all made on Barbados, at over 25 shops in replica chattel houses selling local art, pottery, woodwork, glass products and clothes. There's a café and over Christmas and during busier tourist seasons **Bridgetown Night Market** is held here on Fridays when shops stay open later and there's additional craft, cocktail and food stalls.

Food

Barbados has many supermarkets, convenience stores and fresh produce markets, and at several village fish markets around the island you can get fish cleaned and filleted by the vendors.

Cheapside Public Market, *Cheapside Rd, Bridgetown, T426 4463. Daily 0700-1700.* Bridgetown's main market is good for fruit and vegetables and is a colourful place to visit (page 28).

The Green Monkey Chocolatier, *Quayside Centre, Highway 7, Rockley, Christ Church, T435 5567, Mon-Sat 1000-1800, Sun 1100-1900; and Limegrove Lifestyle Centre, Holetown, St James, T427 5567, Mon-Sat 1000-1800 and in the airport departures lounge, T273 5567, daily 0600-until last flight; www.thegreenmonkeychocolatier. com.* Expensive but deliciously decadent handcrafted artisanal chocolates, rum truffles, French macarons, eclairs, brioches, chocolate-dipped marshmallows and jams and marmalades. The Limegrove branch has a small café serving coffee, gourmet teas, hot chocolate and champagne.

Hastings Farmers Market, *ArtSplash Centre, Highway 7, Hastings, Christ Church, T228 0776. Wed, Sat and Sun 0800-1400.* Organic fruit, vegetables and eggs, freshly baked breads and pastries, prepared Bajan meals, plus arts and crafts and handmade soaps and lotions. The **ArtSplash Centre** (*www. artsplashbarbados.com*) has a children's play park with 2 zip-lines and a café, and is free on market days.

Holders House Farmers Market, *Holders Hse, Holders Hill, St James, T844 1729, see Facebook. Sun 0900-1400.* Set in the grounds of the beautiful historic Holders House (page 46) and overlooking one of the Sandy Lane golf courses, stalls sell arts and crafts, organic farm produce, and food products such as gourmet cheeses, jams, jellies and chutneys.

Massy Stores, *www.massystoresbb.com.* The best of the supermarkets (Massy Stores are Caribbean-wide), always well stocked and have bakeries, deli counters and pharmacies. The larger branches are in Holetown, Oistins, Warrens, Worthing, Six Cross Roads, Sheraton Mall and Sky Mall, and are generally open Mon-Thu 0800-2000, Fri-Sat 0800-2100, Sun 0900-1400.

Shopping malls

Limegrove Lifestyle Centre, *Highway 1, Holetown, St James, T620 5463, www. limegrove.com. Mon-Sat 1000-1800, Sun Dec-Jan only 1000-1700; restaurants later.* An attractive and upscale complex with shops selling luxury brands, as well as cafés, bars, a cinema, art gallery and spa.

Sheraton Mall, *Sargeants Village, Christ Church, T437 0970, www.sheratonmall.com. Mon-Sat 0900-2000.* Immediately off the ABC Highway, the largest mall on the island with over 120 shops, banks, a food court and a multiplex cinema. Roughly a 10-min drive north of St Lawrence Gap, the mall offers a free shuttle service from hotels on the south coast (phone to organize pick-up) and it's on several bus routes.

Sky Mall, *Haggatt Hall, St Michael, T537 8004, www.skymall.bb. Mon-Sat 0900-2000.*

At the JTC Ramsay roundabout on the ABC Highway, also known as the Bussa roundabout after the large statue there. An assortment of general shops, a food court and a large **Massy Stores** supermarket.

What to do

Cricket
Kensington Oval, *President Kennedy Dr, Bridgetown, T536 0351/2, www.kensingtonoval.org*. Cricket in the Caribbean is a game played to a backdrop of rapturous music and joyous partying, and in front of the world's most knowledgeable spectators, who can provide a breakdown of tactics and techniques (or their absence) in West Indian batting. Bridgetown's historic Oval was established in 1882, and today's seating capacity is 11,000; there's also a large grassy hill for picnics. For fixtures, check the websites of the Barbados Cricket Association (*www.barbadoscricket.org*) or Cricket West Indies (*www.windiescricket.com*). For information about tours of the Oval, and the nearby **Cricket Legends of Barbados** museum, see page 29.

Cycling
Bike Caribbean, *Mirabelle Apartments, St Lawrence Gap, Christ Church, T269 2811, www.bikecaribbeantours.com*. Run by Randy Licorish who can organize bike tours just about anywhere on the island from 2 to 6 hrs using mountain, road or electric bikes; US$65-250 per person. Examples are along the cliffs and bays on the extreme north coast; a combination of hiking and biking along the old railway track on the east coast; or a gentler ride alongside the south coast beaches. Also rents out mountain/road bikes from the shop in St Lawrence Gap (*Mon-Fri 0900-1400*) from US$25 a day with helmets; weekly rates available and can deliver.

Diving
For the best dive locations, see page 17. Scuba-diving to reefs or wrecks can be arranged with a number of companies on the south and west coasts who will organize transfers from hotels. Expect to pay in the region of US$90 for a 1-tank dive, US$160 for a 2-tank dive, US$115 for a night dive, US$135 for a PADI Discover scuba/resort course, and US$550-650 for a PADI Open Water course. In the event of a diving emergency, the Barbados hyperbaric chamber is at the Barbados Defence Force Headquarters, St Ann's Fort, Bridgetown, T436 5483.

Barbados Blue, *Hilton Barbados Resort, Needhams Point, Bridgetown, T434 5764, www.divebarbadosblue.com*.
Dive Hightide, *Coral Reef Club, Porters, 1.6 km north of Holetown, St James, T432 0931, www.divehightide.com*.
G Fish Watersports, *Aquatic Gap, Barbados Cruising Club, Bridgetown, T287 5289, www.gfishbarbados.com*.
Reefers & Wreckers, *Gibbes, St Peter, T422 5450, www.scubadiving.bb*.
Roger's Scuba Shack, *Bay St, Bridgetown, T436 3483, www.rogersscubashack.com*.
Sandals Aqua Centre, *Bridgetown, St Michael, T271 0791, www.sandals.com/scuba*.
Seahorse Divers, *St Lawrence Main Rd, Christ Church, T230 7485, www.seahorsediversbb.com*.
Spearfishing & Freediving Barbados, *Aquatic Gap, Barbados Cruising Club, Bridgetown, T230 8580, www.spearfishingbarbados.com*.
West Side Scuba Centre, *The Boatyard, Bay St, Bridgetown, T262 1029, www.westsidescuba.com*.

Fishing
The Atlantic waters off Barbados are ideal for fishing barracuda, blue and white marlin, yellowfin tuna, sailfish, wahoo and dolphin fish (dorado or mahi mahi). Fishing is particularly good Jan-Apr when all these are in season. The Barbados Game Fishing Association runs fishing events including the Barbados International Game Fishing Tournament in mid-Apr at Port St Charles.

The operators listed here, along with many other charter boats for game fishing, are lined up along the Careenage, Bridgetown, so you can inspect the goods before deciding who to call. Trips include tackle and bait, drinks and snacks, lunch on full-day trips, and some organize a stop on a beach or a swim with the turtles. For 6 people, expect to pay around US$650 for 4 hrs, US$1000/6 hrs and US$1200/8 hrs. Ask the operators about shared charters, which, if available, start from US$225 per person/4 hrs.

Blue Fin Fishing, *T253 1267, www.bluefinfishingbarbados.com.*
Cannon Charters, *T424 6107, www.fishingbarbados.com.*
Legacy Fishing Charters, *T822 8228, www.letsgofishingbarbados.com.*

Golf

An 18-hole round costs from US$165 to US$255 and more, but most clubs offer 3- to 7-day deals for people on holiday and there are low-season and group discounts. All rent out clubs and golf carts.

Apes Hill Club, *Apes Hill, St James, T538 0590, https://apeshill.com/golf.* A beautiful and challenging par-72 18-hole championship course high up in the hills with a tremendous view of the west coast and an upmarket country club.

Barbados Golf Club, *Durants, Christ Church, T538 4653, www.barbadosgolfclub.com.* A public par-72 18-hole course with 5 lakes, clubhouse, pro shop and driving range; a 5-min drive from Oistins on Highway 7, so handy for the south coast.

Rockley Golf & Country Club, *Rockley, Christ Church, T435 7873, www.rockleygolfclub.com.* An informal and less expensive par-70 9-hole course, with bar, restaurant and pro shop; lessons are available.

Royal Westmoreland, *Westmoreland, St James, T419 7242, www.royalwestmoreland.com.* A par-72 18-hole course spread over a 194 ha (480 acre) hilly site with views over the west coast. To play here you must be staying in one of the villas or at a hotel with an access agreement, or be the guest of a member. Clubhouse, pro shop and driving range.

Sandy Lane, *St James, T444 2000, www.sandylane.com.* 3 golf courses; the 9-hole **Old Nine**, and the Tom Fazio designed 18-hole **Country Club** and **Green Monkey**. The latter is carved from an old stone quarry and is exclusive to Sandy Lane guests only. Golf carts are fitted with GPS, there are caddies, driving range and a fine clubhouse where Tiger Woods got married in 2004.

Hiking

Barbados may not be very high, but there are numerous opportunities to hike unguided through sugar cane fields, gullies, rural communities and isolated coasts. A recommended hike is along part of the old railway line on the east coast (see box, page 64).

Barbados Hiking Association, *see Facebook.* In association with the Barbados National Trust, the Barbados Hiking Association organizes 3 hr Sun hikes at 0600 and groups are separated into 4 speeds or capabilities: 'stop and stare', 8-10 km; 'medium', 10-15 km; 'brisk medium', 15-20 km; and 'grin and bear', more than 20 km and for those who are able to run up and down hills. On most Suns 'stop and stare' hikes also go at 1530 and moonlight hikes at 1730. They start from various locations around the island and are free, but donations to the Barbados National Trust are welcome. Additional fee-paying special hikes throughout the year include the 5K Safari (Jan), Great Train Hike (Feb), and Hill Challenge (May). Schedules are posted on the Facebook page or pick one up at the Barbados National Trust office in Wildey (page 78).

Hike Barbados, *T230 4818, www.hikingbarbados.com.* Highly regarded and entertaining Stephen Mendes knows Barbados intimately and offers enjoyable guided scenic walks of 3-16 km for US$250-350 per group up to 5, excluding pick-up.

Horse riding
Ocean Echo Stables, *New Castle, St John, T433 6772, www.oceanechoadventures.com*. This stables and farm near Martin's Bay on the east coast offer a number of activities including horse riding; from US$80 for 1½ hrs down to Bath Beach suitable for beginners, to US$140 for 3 hrs taking in Codrington College and Conset Bay for experienced riders, and there's also a 1½ hr full moon ride, US$125. Additionally a moderate 2 hr guided hike follows the old railway line from Martin's Bay to Bath Beach, US$50, and the stables has a yoga *shala* on a clifftop with terrific sea views, US$50 or US$30 for 3 or more for 1 hr with a qualified yoga instructor. The property also has 3 peaceful self-catering apartments for rent (**$$-$**).

Polo
The first polo match on Barbados was played in 1884; British cavalry officers had brought the sport with them and it was a game that suited the Bajan lifestyle as a number of wealthy plantation owners had their own stables. Matches were originally played at the Garrison Savannah but today there are two world-class polo fields on the island. It remains the sport of the affluent elite but, like horse racing (see box, page 37), polo is a wonderful afternoon's entertainment for spectators. The season starts just after Christmas and runs through to May. You can watch while sipping a cup of tea or a glass of wine and there is always a lively lime afterwards. There are usually 2 matches held from about 1500 on match days; admission is around US$10, and children under 10 are free.

Apes Hill Polo Club, *Apes Hill, St James, T262 3282, www.apeshillpolo.biz*.
Barbados Polo Club, *Holders Hill, St James, T432 1802, https://barbadospolo.club*.

Running
Barbados Hash House Harriers, *www.barbadoshash.com*. Every Sat the Hash (sometimes 100-strong) have a 1-2 hr fun run/walk starting from a different location each week, followed by a barbecue and drinks or a meal at a beach bar. Events are posted on the website and it costs US$2 to participate.
Run Barbados, *www.visitbarbados.org/runbarbados-marathon-weekend*. Held in early Dec and open to all, this consists of a 'Fun Mile', 5 km, 10 km, a half marathon, and a full individual and relay team marathon. The 'out and back' mostly flat route starts on the Bay Street Esplanade overlooking Carlisle Bay. Fees range from US$20 to US$100.

Sailing
A number of outfits in Bridgetown offer lunchtime and sunset cruises on sleek catamarans, many of which are based at the Careenage while others are at Shallow Draught off Mighty Grynner (Spring Garden) Highway, 1.3 km north of Bridgetown Cruise Terminal. If you pre-book, transport from hotels is included in the rates. Each takes a maximum of 12-14 for a comfortable and friendly tour of the west coast, stopping to snorkel over a couple of wrecks and swimming with turtles. Lunch cruises usually go from 0930 and return at 1430 and cost in the region of US$115-150, children (3-12) US$80-115, under 3s free. They include a Bajan-style buffet lunch and unlimited drinks, including rum punch. Sunset cruises are 1500-1900, US$100-150/US$55-115 depending on the type of meal you get – finger food or a full dinner plus drinks. There's also the option of booking a private charter for families/groups.

Calabaza Sailing Cruises, *at the Careenage, Bridgetown, T826 4048, www.sailcalabaza.com*.
Cool Runnings Catamaran Cruises, *at the Careenage, Bridgetown, T436 0911, www.coolrunningsbarbados.com*.
Elegance Catamaran Cruises, *at the Careenage, Bridgetown, T830 4218, www.elegancebarbados.com*.

El Tigre Catamaran Sailing Cruises, *at the Careenage, Bridgetown, T417 7245, www.eltigrecruises.com.*
Silver Moon Catamaran Cruises, *Shallow Draught, Bridgetown, T435 5285, www.silvermoonbarbados.com.*
Small Cats Catamaran Sailing Cruises Barbados, *at the Careenage, Bridgetown, T421 6419, www.smallcatscruises.com.*
Tiami Catamaran Cruises, *Shallow Draught, Bridgetown, T430 0900, https://tiamicatamaransbarbados.com.*

Stand-up paddle boarding (SUP)

There are lots of good locations for SUPing in the quieter bays of the south and west coasts. Many of the resorts have boards for their guests and it's great for all ages and beginners.

Paddle Barbados, *Barbados Cruising Club, Aquatic Gap, off Bay St, Bridgetown, T249 2787, www.paddlebarbados.com. Daily 1000-1800.* Rents out boards for US$30 for 1 hr or US$40 for 4 hrs, which includes brief instruction, and also offers SUP lessons and a tour in Carlisle Bay, 1½ hrs US$70, and SUP yoga sessions for US$40. Also rents out snorkelling gear, boogie boards and inflatable kayaks from their base at the **Barbados Cruising Club**, and delivers/picks up SUPs and regular surf boards to your hotel if you want to rent for a few days; from US$40 per day.

Submarine tours

Atlantis Submarines Barbados, *Shallow Draught, off Mighty Grynner (Spring Garden) Highway, 1.3 km north of Bridgetown Cruise Terminal, Bridgetown, T436 8929, www.barbados.atlantissubmarines.com. Up to 7 departures daily – check website for times, daytime tour US$120, children (12 and under, but above 92 cm tall) US$60, night tour US$130/US$60, stated prices include online advance booking discount.* For those who want to see underwater without getting wet, a voyage on the 48-seater, air-conditioned, 20 m long, 73-tonne Atlantis III Submarine is an expensive but thrilling alternative and great for kids. The port-holed craft submerges to the ocean bed at a maximum depth of 45 m; the day dives concentrate on the numerous fish, turtles and reef life and take you to a shipwreck, while the night dive also illuminates the corals and predator fish with coloured spotlights (Barbados is the only place in the world besides Grand Cayman offering nocturnal submarine tours). The whole trip lasts 1 hr 30 mins, but begins with a short video and then the boat ride from the dock to the submarine and back, so the underwater time is about 45 mins. Atlantis operates more than a dozen such submersibles worldwide and has carried almost 20 million passengers on more than half a million dives to date. They have been operating on Barbados for almost 40 years and have a good safety record.

Surfing

For the best surf spots, see page 19.
For further information on surfing events on Barbados, check the Facebook page of the **Barbados Surfing Association**. Most of the surf schools on the island are mobile; they take you to where the waves are best. Surfing lessons are usually somewhere along the south coast, and free south coast hotel pick-ups are often included. Most offer 2 hr group lessons, US$60-80, and packages of 3 lessons and a board for a week, US$180-200. All offer board rentals for around US$15 per 2 hrs, US$25-35 per day and US$125-150 per week (price depends on whether they are fun short boards or quality long boards) and most operators will deliver to your accommodation. Check with your airline how much it costs to bring your board with you to Barbados and compare costs. For repairs and to buy or rent gear, as well as surfing and SUP tuition, the **Dread or Dead** surf shop and school is on Hastings Main Rd (Highway 7), Christ Church, T228 4785, www.dreadordead.com, Mon-Sat 0900-1600, Sun 1000-1300.

Barry's Surf School Barbados, *T256 3906, www.surfing-barbados.com*.
Boosy's Surf School, *T267 3182, www.learntosurfbarbados.com*.
Burkie's Surf School, *T832 1664, www.blog.surfbarbados.net*.
Paddle Barbados, *T249 2787, www.paddlebarbados.com*.
Ride the Tide Surf School, *T234 2361, www.ridethetidebarbados.com*.
SurfInBarbados Surf School, *T826 6672, www.surfinbarbados.com*.
Zed's Surfing Adventures, *T231 5251, www.zedssurfing.com*.

Tour operators

Cruise-ship passengers are given a taste of the island by being whisked round in about 6 hrs. These tours include stops at Cherry Tree Hill and Morgan Lewis Windmill, a drive through the Scotland District to the beach at Bathsheba on the east coast and St John's Church, and then perhaps a visit to the Flower Forest Botanical Gardens, Gun Hill Signal Station or Sunbury Plantation Great House. These tours can seem rushed, but are fine if you want a drive around the island to see the nicest views and don't want to hire a car. Costs are around US$100-150, children (under 12) half price and include lunch. As well as the Bridgetown Cruise Terminal, operators will pick up from south and west coast hotels. Tour operators also offer more detailed tours to sights, or a combination of places, including Bridgetown and the Garrison, Welchman Hall Gully, Harrison's Cave Eco-Adventure Park, St Nicholas Abbey, Hunte's Gardens, Barbados Wildlife Reserve, Bathsheba and the east coast and more. Expect to pay from US$80-110 for a 4 hr tour up to US$130-180 for a full day 7-8 hr tour, children (under 12) half price, depending on what the arrangements are: entry fees, distances and whether lunch is included. Explore the tour operator websites for ideas. Another option for a group/family is to charter a vehicle and guide and make up your own itinerary (most tours are by small 8- to 12-seater minibus). Finally, you could also find a taxi driver you like, or get a hotel to recommend one (some of them make very good and entertaining tour guides) and set off on your own; the hourly rate is US$45-50 and many taxis are in fact minibuses.

Beautiful Barbados, *T231 2932, www.beautifulbarbadostoursandexcursions.com*.
Carson's Taxi & Tours Service, *T240 5339, see Facebook*
Emmanuel Tours, *T232 0711, www.emmanueltoursbarbados.com*.
Island Safari Barbados, *T429 5337, www.islandsafari.bb*.
RCR Tours, *T230 5357, see Facebook*
SunTours Barbados, *T434 8430, www.suntoursbarbados.com*.
Williams Tours Barbados, *T427 1043, www.williamstoursbarbados.com*.

Windsurfing and kitesurfing

For the best places to windsurf and kitesurf, see page 19. Many of the resorts have equipment for their guests and staff can provide instruction.

deAction, *Silver Sands, Christ Church, T428 2027, www.briantalma.pro*. Run by Brian Talma, a Barbadian watersports legend, who can rent out boards as well as organize instruction in surfing, windsurfing, kitesurfing and SUPing at Silver Sands and Long Beach, where he also offers self-catering apartments (**$$-$**).
Endless Kiteboarding, *Silver Rock, Christ Church, T251 7190, www.endlesskiteboarding.com*. Run by IKO instructor Roland Boyce, offers 2 hr beginners' kite lessons from US$150 per person for groups of 2-4, or US$95 per hr for private 1-to-1 instruction, while 2 hr group beginners' windsurfing lessons are US$80, 1-to-1 US$60 per hour, and he rents out gear.

Background

A sprint through history 99
Modern Barbados 101

History

A sprint through history

350-1500 The first settlers of the island are believed to be people from mainland South America: the Amerindians (350-650), followed by the Arawak Indians (around 800), and the Caribs who invaded and forced the Arawaks off during the 1200s. The Caribs later left when the Europeans sailed into the Caribbean region, and by the early 1500s the island was uninhabited.

1536 Portuguese explorer Pedro a Campos discovered the island en route to Brazil and named it Los Barbados ('the bearded ones'), possibly after the island's fig trees (see box, page 40). The Portuguese didn't stay but left behind some wild pigs, which bred successfully and provided meat for the first English settlers.

1625-1627 Captain John Powell landed on Barbados and claimed the uninhabited island for England. Two years later, his brother Captain Henry Powell landed with a party of 80 settlers and 10 slaves. King Charles I gave permission to colonize the island, and the group established the first European settlement, Jamestown, on the west coast at what is now Holetown.

1639 Governor Henry Hawley founded the House of Assembly. Some 40,000 white settlers (about 1% of the population of England) arrived, mostly small cotton and tobacco farmers.

1643 Commercial production of sugar began, with plants introduced from Brazil by Dutch Jews, who also brought capital, credit, technology and markets.

1651-1652 After the execution of King Charles I (1649), Oliver Cromwell sent a fleet to take over Royalist Barbados but his forces were held at bay for six months. The stalemate with Cromwell was resolved with the signing of the Articles of Agreement, later recognized as the Charter of Barbados by the English Parliament.

1650-1670 A sugar revolution saw the consolidation of small farms into large plantations. Most of the original white-settler smallholders left and the plantations were instead owned by the 'landed gentry' who arrived from England, and there was large-scale importation of slave labour from Africa.

1700 By the turn of this century most of the forests had been cleared for sugar; there were more than 800 sugar mills and the population was put at 15,000 whites and 50,000 enslaved blacks.

1751 George Washington visited Barbados to enjoy its healthy environment; this was his only journey outside the American mainland.

1807 Britain abolished the African slave trade, but not slavery. Barbados exported locally bred slaves to other colonies.

1816 Bussa's Rebellion, when 20,000 slaves from over 70 plantations demonstrated and destroyed sugar cane fields. Several hundred were killed in battle or hanged afterwards, but no plantation owners or their families died. Signal stations were subsequently built across the island to give advance warning of further rebellions.

1834 The UK Parliament passed the Emancipation Bill with slaves to undergo a four-year apprenticeship period before full emancipation. Men continued to work a 45-hour week without pay in exchange for living in the tiny huts provided by the plantation owners.

1838 Slavery was abolished with full freedom at the end of the apprenticeship period. Barbadian slave owners were compensated with average payments of £20 13s 8d per slave.

1840s Barbadian labourers earned half that of Trinidadians and were the lowest paid in the Caribbean (except Montserrat). Sugar prices fell with greater competition worldwide.

1894 Sugar exports were 50,958 tons, 97% of total exports, but market share was declining because of absentee plantation owners, lack of capital investment and technological improvement, and competition from European sugar beet.

1898 The Windward Islands Hurricane devastated Barbados, with over 5000 homes destroyed, 40,000-45,000 people left homeless, and the sugar cane plantations suffering crippling damage.

1904-1914 About 60,000 workers went to Panama to help construct the canal – 20,000 in 1909 alone.

1923 20,000 migrants left for New York.

1930s Effects of the worldwide depression were felt on Barbados, with unemployment, poor working conditions, falling wages and higher imported food prices. The next events of historical significance involved the advent of labour unions.

1937 Colonial authorities arrested and deported Clement Payne, a trade union organizer from Trinidad who spread word of labour unrest and riots in neighbouring islands and Marcus Garvey's teachings on pan-Africanism. Riots followed, with police shooting and killing 14, wounding 47 and arresting over 400.

1939-1945 The Second World War; there was a reprieve for the sugar industry because of the disruption of beet growing in Europe but U-boat activity limited food imports to the Caribbean islands. The trade union movement continued to gain momentum and the Barbados Labour Party (BLP) was formed, headed by lawyer Grantley Adams (1898-1971), who had represented Clement Payne in his appeal against deportation.

1945 The West India Royal Commission, chaired by Lord Moyne, produced a damning report on neglect and deprivation in the British Caribbean, describing squalid and unhealthy slums and the dire state of education and health provision.

1947 The BLP won the general elections.

1954 Grantley Adams became the first Premier of Barbados under a new system of ministerial government.

1955 Hurricane Janet caused 38 deaths and severe destruction of homes and infrastructure (an estimated US$5 million at the time). Since Janet, the island hasn't experienced any significant hurricanes although it is hit by milder tropical storms; nonetheless, in 2021 Hurricane Elsa caused extensive damage but no serious injuries or deaths.

1958-1962 In 1958 all the British Caribbean islands agreed to create the West Indies Federation, with the intention of establishing a political unit that would become independent from Britain as a single state; Grantley Adams served as its first and only

Premier. Before that could happen, Trinidad and Tobago and Jamaica gained their own independence in 1962 and the federation collapsed. The remaining states once again became self-governing colonies of Britain.

1960s A tourism boom began on Barbados with the introduction of affordable long-haul jet aircraft. (Tourism has begun in earnest during the 1950s when it became a destination for the wealthy, whose lavish lifestyle is still visible primarily along the west coast.)

1961 Internal autonomy was granted and Errol Walton Barrow (1920-1987) of the Democratic Labour Party (DLP) replaced Grantley Adams as Premier and the DLP took control of government.

1966 After several years of peaceful and democratic progress, Barbados became an independent state and formally joined the Commonwealth of Nations on 30 November 1966. Barrow became Barbados' first Prime Minister, an office he kept until 1976.

1976-2018 After independence, Barbados' politics operated within a framework of a constitutional monarchy, under Queen Elizabeth II, who appointed a governor-general to be her representative on Barbados and a government of two houses: an elected House of Assembly and an appointed Senate. Power has alternated between the Democratic Labour Party (DLP) and the Barbados Labour Party (BLP). In 1976, Tom Adams (1931-1985) of the DLP – and Sir Grantley Adams's son – became Prime Minister and served until 1985.

2018-2021 Mia Mottley, leader of the BLP, became the first female and eighth Prime Minister of Barbados. She was a strong supporter of Barbados becoming a republic and removing the British sovereign as head of state; parliament amended the constitution in October 2021.

2021-present day Dame Sandra Mason, the final governor-general of Barbados, took office in 2021 as the country's first president when Barbados ceased to be a constitutional monarchy and became a republic. The Queen sent a message of congratulations and Prince Charles attended the ceremony on Barbados. In January 2022, Mottley and the BLP won a landslide victory in snap elections, securing all 30 seats in the Assembly for the second consecutive time.

Modern Barbados

Barbados gained independence in 1966 after more than three centuries of British rule. In the 18th century, when slavery was at its peak, Africans outnumbered their British masters by three to one, and sugar provided a livelihood for everyone. But Barbados didn't just have a population of slave owners and oppressed slaves; there were also free but impoverished white indentured servants that had been banished from England, and a settled Jewish population fleeing from persecution. As such, unlike many other Caribbean islands, there was slightly better treatment of slaves by their masters and fewer slave uprisings (also partly attributed to the large British military and police presence). However, resentment grew, particularly after the Haitian Revolution and when emancipation was being debated in England. In 1816 the slaves rose up and burned the cane fields and plantation buildings in a show of defiance – an event still acknowledged today. The rebellion leader, Bussa, is one of the 10 National Heroes of Barbados.

Slavery was finally abolished in 1838 but not much changed for the blacks, who ended up as very cheap labour and were unable to purchase land of their own. The white plantocracy remained in control of all productive land, becoming allied to a rising merchant class in

BACKGROUND
Music

No visitor to Barbados can fail to notice the extent to which music pervades daily life. Whether it is reggae pounding out from a passing ZR van or gospel music being belted out in a church, Bajan rhythm is inescapable. The West Africans dragged to the island as slaves brought with them tastes in music and dance which are still evident today. This intensity of sound and beat has produced many musicians, several of whom have become world famous, such as calypsonians The Mighty Gabby, The Mighty Grynner and Red Plastic Bag, reggae vocalist David Kirton, jazz saxophonist Arturo Tappin, R&B singer Jackie Opel, and soca artists Alison Hinds, Krosfyah, Rupee and Square One. And then there's Rihanna…

Calypso is the music for which Barbados is most famous, although it was originally developed in Trinidad. Calypsonians (or kaisonians, as the more historically minded call them) are the commentators, champions and sometime conscience of the people. It combines a mixture of African, French and, eventually, British, Spanish and even East Indian influences, and dates back to Trinidad's first 'shantwell', Gros Jean, late in the 18th century. Since then it has evolved into a popular, potent force, with both men and women (also children, of late) battling for the Calypso Monarch's crown during Crop Over, Barbados' carnival (see box, page 16). The season's calypso songs blast from sound systems all over the islands and visitors should ask locals to interpret the sometimes witty and often scurrilous lyrics, for they are a fascinating introduction to the state of the nation. There are also 'rapso' artists, fusing calypso and rap music, and 'chutney', an Indian version of calypso, is fused with soca to create 'chutney soca'.

Bridgetown so as to form an entrenched elite with total financial and political power. Poverty ground down the working class, whether they were black or white (the latter were descended from indentured labourers and deported convicts, and were known by the derogatory term 'Red Legs'). Tens of thousands left the country to work on the Panama Canal and those who made money and survived returned to form the nucleus of a black middle class. Resentment grew again at neglect by Britain, poor wages, poor housing and poor education, and in the 1930s there were riots. Out of conflict, the seeds of a labour movement grew, led by Barbadians such as Grantley Adams and Errol Walton Barrow (both now National Heroes of Barbados), who went on to found the two main political parties and steer the country to independence.

Just as the political landscape has changed, so there has also been a shift in the economy. Like the other Caribbean islands to the west, sugar is no longer king but has been deposed by tourism, and since the 1960s, resorts and golf courses have been constructed on land formerly devoted to sugar cane. While this kind of continual development is detrimental to the island's ecology and environment (although the plantation owners initially stripped the island of forests and eroded the coastlines), this move to a service economy has been largely successful.

The tourism sector on Barbados recovered remarkably quickly after the Covid-19 pandemic, with 2024 and 2025 seeing all-time record numbers of visitors. There are now some 1.5 million tourists annually (of which more than half are cruise passengers); tourism accounts for about 17% of GDP and directly or indirectly supports at least 33% of local employment. Unlike some other islands that are highly reliant on the US market,

Steel pan music was again developed in Trinidad in the early 20th century from the carnival tamboo-bamboo bands, which made creative use of tins, dustbins and pans plus lengths of bamboo for percussion instruments. By the end of the Second World War some ingenious souls discovered that huge oil drums could be converted into expressive instruments, their top surfaces tuned to all ranges and depths (eg the ping pong, or soprano pan embraces 28 to 32 notes, including both the diatonic and chromatic scales). Aside from the pannists playing the steel pans, bands also include rhythm musicians playing saxophones and trumpets.

Reggae is tremendously popular across the Caribbean and originated in Jamaica in the 1960s. On Barbados it's played everywhere, all day, all night, and the Barbados Reggae Festival is held in April (page 14). However, Barbadians like to vary their reggae so there is also a fusion of reggae and soca, known as ragga-soca, which has a faster rhythm than reggae but slower than up-tempo soca.

Tuk is one of the most traditional forms of folk music, having its origins in slave culture of the 17th century, and an important means of expression for the black masses on Barbados. The name is derived from an old Scottish word 'touk', meaning the beat/tap of a drum, but it was banned by the English as subversive; plantation overseers believed that the drums were used to send messages, and it had to wait until after emancipation to resurface officially. Since the revival of Crop Over in 1974, tuk bands have flourished. The instruments used are the kettle drum, bass drum and tin flute, and the music is lively, with a pulsating rhythm influenced by British regimental band music as well as African dances. It is 'jump-up' music, used at holiday times and carnival accompanying masquerades.

Barbados attracts a mix of visitors, with about 38% coming from North America and a similar proportion from the UK; most of the rest come from elsewhere in the Caribbean and western Europe. Its appeal is an attractive and accessible destination, and (non-cruise) repeat visitors have been 40%. It has, however, like all popular tourist destinations, suffered major economic dips; notably the general global recession of 2008-2009 and the Covid-19 pandemic. Nevertheless, holidaymakers go home with nothing but good things to say about the friendliness of Barbadians and the excellent – if sometimes slow (this is the Caribbean after all) – service they received in hotels and restaurants.

Because Barbados lies upwind from the main Caribbean island arc, it was hard to attack from the sea, so it never changed hands in the colonial wars of the 17th and 18th centuries. There is no French, Dutch or Spanish influence to speak of in the language, cooking or culture. Today, the more obvious outside influences on the Barbadian way of life are North American, from fast-food chains to TV programmes. However, Afro-Caribbean roots are of paramount importance to Barbadians, reflected in the rhythm of music and festivals like Crop Over, as well as food derived from slave ration staples brought over from Africa.

One withstanding influence from Britain that sport-mad Barbadians will not shake off, however, is cricket, and everyone has an opinion on the latest matches, the team selection and the state of the West Indies side. In the rare event that you are stuck for a topic of conversation, you can rely on cricket to start a lively debate and a cricket match is symbolic of the way Barbadians approach life – with fun, drama and huge enjoyment in the sport amid a cacophony of noise.

Practicalities

Getting there 105
Getting around 109
Essentials A-Z 112

Getting there

Air

Barbados' popularity as a tourist destination means regular flights from Europe and North America and you can often pick up good-value deals on package holidays; combining flights with a hotel can often work out cheaper than booking each separately, and airport-to-hotel transfers are usually included. Barbados is also the hub of the Eastern Caribbean region and has good connections for some island-hopping by air. **Grantley Adams International Airport** ⓘ *T536 1300, www.gaia.bb*, is 16 km east of Bridgetown, near the resorts on the south coast and connected to the west coast beaches by the Adams Barrow Cummins (ABC) Highway which bypasses the capital. Flights to Barbados are heavily booked in high season (mid-December to mid-April), especially at Christmas and Easter, and also for Crop Over (June-early August).

Flights from the UK

The scheduled carriers to Barbados from the UK are **British Airways** ⓘ *www.britishairways.com*, and **Virgin Atlantic** ⓘ *www.virginatlantic.com*, who both fly daily from London Heathrow. Both have connecting services to/from other UK airports and mainland Europe. In high season (November-May), **Aer Lingus** ⓘ *www.aerlingus.com*, flies three times per week from Manchester, and **TUI** ⓘ *www.tui.co.uk*, flies at least once a week from London Gatwick and several regional airports, including Belfast, Birmingham, Cardiff, Glasgow, Manchester and Newcastle.

> **Tip...**
> Direct flying time to Barbados from UK airports is 7½-9 hours; Frankfurt is 11½ hours; Miami is 3½ hours; New York 5 hours; and Toronto 4 hours.

Flights from the rest of Europe

In high season (October-March), **KLM** ⓘ *www.klm.com*, has direct flights from Amsterdam three times a week. **Condor** ⓘ *www.condor.com*, flies once a week from Frankfurt (and seasonally also from Dusseldorf) via either Grenada or Tobago, as do **Discover Airlines** ⓘ *www.discover-airlines.com*, which flies seasonally in November-March. Europeans also have the option of flying to another island and connecting to Barbados using a regional airline such as **Caribbean Airlines** or **interCaribbean**. For instance, **Air France** ⓘ *www.airfrance.com*, **Air Caraïbes** ⓘ *www.aircaraibes.com*, and **Corsair** ⓘ *www.corsair.fr*, fly from Paris to the French Antilles islands such as Guadeloupe and Martinique, and **KLM** ⓘ *www.klm.com*, flies year-round to Aruba and Saint Martin/Sint Maarten among other Caribbean destinations. Connecting flights from European cities also go via North America; Miami in the USA with **American Airlines** or Toronto in Canada with **Air Canada** or **WestJet**, for example.

Flights from North America

American Airlines ⓘ *www.aa.com*, flies to Barbados from New York, Miami and Charlotte, **Delta** ⓘ *www.delta.com* from Atlanta, and **JetBlue** ⓘ *www.jetblue.com*, from New York, all connecting from numerous cities in the USA. **Air Canada** ⓘ *www.aircanada.com*, and **WestJet** ⓘ *www.westjet.com*, fly from Toronto, both connecting from several cities in Canada. Again, an option is to fly to a nearby island; for example **Caribbean Airlines** ⓘ *www.caribbean-airlines.com*, flies from New York, Orlando, Fort Lauderdale, Miami and Toronto to Trinidad, with onward connections to Barbados, while **Delta** ⓘ *www.delta.com*, flies from Atlanta to Saint Martin/Sint Maarten, St Vincent, St Lucia and Turks and Caicos, and from New York to the Dominican Republic and Puerto Rico, from where **interCaribbean Airways,** ⓘ *www.intercaribbean.com*, connect to Barbados.

Flights from South America

interCaribbean Airways ⓘ *www.intercaribbean.com*, has a direct flight to Barbados from Georgetown in Guyana, and **Caribbean Airlines** flies to Barbados via Trinidad from Caracas in Venezuela, Georgetown and Ogle in Guyana and Paramaribo in Suriname.

Flights from Australia, New Zealand and South Africa

There are no direct flights and connections must be made through the UK or North America.

Flights from the Caribbean

Caribbean Airlines ⓘ *www.caribbean-airlines.com*, connects Barbados to its hubs in Trinidad and Jamaica, as well as Antigua, Dominica, Martinique, St Lucia and Tobago, and onward connections to other regional islands and destinations in North and South America. Based in the Turks and Caicos Islands, **interCaribbean Airways** ⓘ *www.intercaribbean.com*, has direct flights to/from Barbados, Antigua, Dominica, Grenada, Jamaica, St Kitts, St Lucia and St Vincent, and from its two hubs in the British Virgin Islands and Turks and Caicos, connecting flights to the rest of its network of 20-odd

> **Tip...**
> When booking with an international airline that involves a change on another Caribbean island, it is likely to be on a codeshare agreement with a regional airline and ticketed straight through to Barbados. Flights on the small airlines are generally reliable, but schedules may change and they tend to run on 'island time'. But this has got its advantages too; they could wait for you if an international connection is delayed.

destinations across the Caribbean as far north as Cuba and the Bahamas. **SVG Air** ⓘ *www.flysvgair.com*, and **Mustique Airways** ⓘ *www.mustique.com*, provide a scheduled service between Barbados and St Vincent, Bequia, Canouan, Grenada, Carriacou, and Union Island in the Grenadines, while **Mustique Airways** also touches down on Mustique on request. Private air charter services can be arranged to/from most of the islands with the regional airlines (including **SVG Air**, **Mustique Airways** or Barbados-based **Executive Air** ⓘ *www.eaairlines.com*) for a group taking the maximum number of seats, or for those prepared to pay for all of them, in a small plane seating from seven in a Cessna to 19 in a Twin Otter. It's worth considering the costs as they can be competitive compared with paying for the same number of seats on scheduled flights.

Airport information

The only airport on the island, **Grantley Adams International Airport** ⓘ *Seawell, Christ Church, T536 1300, www.gaia.bb*, is modern and well equipped, and live flight arrival/departure information is on the website. Facilities include free Wi-Fi, ATMs, foreign exchange bureaux, a post office, car-hire agencies (page 110) and quite a wide range of shops including an inbound branch of **Bridgetown Duty Free** in the arrivals terminal (very useful, saves carrying heavy bottles on the plane). At the end of 2024, the airport opened its new Concorde Terminal (repurposed from the former Concorde hangar, which housed a Concorde Experience museum until 2018) to accommodate the growing number of passengers.

Taxis stop just outside customs. Check the noticeboard on the left as you come out of arrivals, as it gives the official taxi fares. Alternatively see ⓘ *www.gaia.bb/ground-transportation/taxi-rates-from-the-airport*. Authorized airport taxis have a yellow sticker on the side and all taxis have licence plates denoted with a ZR. The taxi dispatcher will give you a trip form and advice on fares; drivers may attempt to charge more if you haven't checked. You can pay in Barbados or US dollars cash. Taxis from the airport to the south coast take 15-30 minutes, to Bridgetown 30 minutes, and to the west coast 40-60 minutes. Example fares are Oistins US$20, St Lawrence Gap US$27, Rockley Beach US$30, Bridgetown US$38, Holetown US$60 and Speightstown US$72. Alternatively the airport is served by **pickUP** ⓘ *www.pickupbarbados.com*, Barbados' ride-hailing taxi app that uses only officially registered drivers; you'll be quoted a fare when you order the ride.

> **Tip...**
> There are several food and drinks outlets within the airport terminals, or alternatively just across the car park and airport access road, you can join the taxi drivers at **Pug's Bar & Restaurant** ⓘ *Tom Adams Hwy, T428 0091, Mon-Sat 0700-2300*, for affordable local food including excellent fried chicken and fish and a first/last cold Banks beer at the outside picnic tables.

There is a bus stop just across the car park on the main road, Tom Adams Highway, from where large **Transport Board** buses (blue with striped yellow sides) run every half-hour along the south coast to Bridgetown, or (over the road) to the Crane. An hourly service also goes to Holetown and Speightstown on the west coast. The flat fare is US$2 (but payable in local currency only), and hours of operation are generally 0500-2100. All timetables can be found on the website ⓘ *www.transportboard.com*. Very few flights arrive late at night, but if you are delayed, all the hotels along the south coast are no more than a short taxi ride away.

Sea

There are no ferry services between Barbados and the other Caribbean islands at the time of writing, but a new service is expected to launch soon, connecting seven islands (including Barbados) with passenger, vehicle and cargo services; see Connect Caribe ⓘ *www.connectcaribe.com*. Cruise ships call at the **Bridgetown Cruise Terminal** ⓘ *T434 6100, www.barbadosport.com*, which has capacity for six vessels at a time, and some passengers choose to start, finish or break their cruise on Barbados. The terminal at **Deep Water Harbour**, about 1.5 km northwest of Bridgetown off Princess Alice Highway, has a **tourist information desk** ⓘ *T426 1718, www.visitbarbados.org, open daily 0900-1700 when cruise ships are in port*, souvenir and duty-free shops, cafés, tour operator desks, a post office and free Wi-Fi. There's a dedicated departure area where tour operators, taxis and car-rental companies pick up, and it's a five-minute drive or 20-minute walk to central Bridgetown.

Being on the windward side of the other Lesser Antilles islands, fewer yachts beat their way against the prevailing winds to visit Barbados. Those that do usually arrive after a long passage either from the Canary or Cape Verde islands across the North Atlantic as Barbados is the first landfall, or they come north from Brazil and the South Atlantic. The only cruising area for yachts is along the sheltered west coast; the east coast is rocky and exposed to the Atlantic breakers and should be given a wide berth. The main anchorage is at Carlisle Bay south of Bridgetown, from where dinghies (tender boats) can approach the beaches, and there are dinghy docks at The Boatyard (page 34), a beach club on Brownes Beach, and at both the island's two yacht clubs: **Barbados Yacht Club** and the **Barbados Cruising Club** (page 35). On the northwest coast near Speightstown, **Port St Charles** ⓘ *T419 1000, www.portstcharles.com*, is an upscale luxury marina development with offshore anchorages, berths that can accommodate superyachts up to 76 m (200 ft) long, services like fuel, electricity and water, and a yacht club with restaurant/bar and dinghy dock. The two ports of entry for clearing, immigration and customs are the **Bridgetown Deep Water Harbour** and **Port St Charles** ⓘ *open daily 24 hrs (overtime fees applicable 2200-0600), more information from Barbados Port Inc, T434 6100, www.barbadosport.com*. A clearance out certificate from your last port is required. Once cleared at Deep Water Harbour, yachts are directed to go and anchor in Carlisle Bay. If you want to visit any other areas, including Port St Charles (or Bridgetown and Carlisle Bay from Port St Charles), skippers will need permission from customs and the port authority.

Getting around

Road

At only 34 km long and 22 km wide, the island is fairly small and the terrain is relatively flat, so nowhere takes too long to get to and there's a good choice of transport options. However, away from the main highways on the south and west coasts, the interior rural roads are narrow, winding and poorly signposted, but Barbadians are more than happy to point you in the right direction if you ask. The Adams Barrow Cummins (ABC) Highway cuts inland from the airport to a point between Brighton and Prospect, north of Bridgetown. This road skirts the east edge of the capital, giving access by various roads into the city and to the west and east coasts. Its roundabouts are named after eminent Barbadians, including Sir Garfield Sobers, Errol Barrow and Everton Weekes. The highway and roads into Bridgetown get jammed at rush hour – weekdays 0700-0900 and 1600-1800 – and the city centre is at its worst in the middle of the day. Minibuses and route taxis run around the capital, cheaply and efficiently, but are terribly slow in rush hour when it's often quicker to walk. North of Bridgetown, heading up the west coast, is Highway 1, giving access to all the beach hotels and restaurants. Highway 2A runs parallel inland, allowing rather speedier access to the north of the island. Along the south coast, Highway 7 runs from the south of Bridgetown and links all the coastal resorts to Oistins.

Bus

There are three types of public bus on Barbados and they are cheap, frequent and crowded. Almost all routes radiate in and out of Bridgetown, so while cross-country journeys may be time-consuming, travelling by bus is very easy and can be a lot of fun and a great way to meet Bajan people. On most

> **Tip...**
> Transport Board bus timetables and route finders can be found on the website of the Transport Board: www.transportboard.com.

routes, the first buses depart around 0500 and run until at least 2100; on the more popular routes they run until midnight. Look out for the red, white and black bus-stop signs at the side of the road; out-of-town bus stops are marked simply 'To City' or 'Out of City'. Some of them have shelters with a bench, and solar USB-charging points for phones, but you rarely have to wait too long for a bus on the busier routes.

The large public buses belonging to the government's Transport Board are hard to miss, and are painted blue with striped yellow sides. The latest models are electric, some with a/c and Wi-Fi. The flat fare is B$3.50 per journey anywhere on the island, so if you change buses you pay again. The drivers do not give change so exact fare is required; if you are boarding at a terminal, you can get change from the cashier (0700-2200). The routes cover just about every corner of the island and usefully service many of the tourist attractions, and there are some circuits which work very well; for example: 1) any south coast bus to Oistins, then cross-country bus to the east coast, then direct bus to Bridgetown; 2) any west coast bus to Speightstown, then bus to Bathsheba on the east coast, then direct bus back to Bridgetown.

There are also plenty of privately owned mid-sized minibuses with B licence plates and painted yellow with blue stripes, and smaller route taxis with ZR licence plates and painted white with maroon stripes. Both typically run on the same routes as Transport Board buses, but tend to concentrate on the highly trafficked and populated areas. Flat fares are

> **Tip...**
> If you are moving between hotels on the south coast and the west coast and have luggage, the Transport Board Bridgetown Shuttle (No 51) runs Monday to Saturday roughly every hour between the Fairchild Street Terminal and the Princess Alice Terminal and takes about 10-15 minutes; alternatively take a city minibus or taxi.

the same for any journey, B$3.50, although drivers/conductors can give change if they have it. If hailed down, they will usually stop anywhere on their route (though they are not supposed to); travelling by ZR van in particular is quite an experience as they are known for their high speed, loud music, sudden stops and packing in as many passengers as possible. If you feel unsafe then get off and find another – or wait for a blue **Transport Board** bus.

Buses for the south and east Fairchild Street Terminal for **Transport Board** buses, which is on the south side of the Careenage just over Charles Duncan O'Neal Bridge, and Nursery Drive Minibus and ZR Terminal for other vehicles, which is just across Constitution River from Fairchild Street.

Buses for the west and north Princess Alice Terminal for **Transport Board** buses, which is on Princess Alice Highway on the way to the Deep Water Harbour, and Cheapside Minibus and ZR Terminal for other vehicles, which is to the north on Cheapside.

Car

Having your own car, if only for a couple days, is highly recommended to get to attractions and restaurants and it's a great way to carry around beach gear and picnics for impromptu stops. The network of minor roads criss-crossing the island can be a little confusing and there are plenty of ways to get lost, but Barbados is an enjoyable destination for a bit of a ramble in the interior, distances aren't great, and it won't take long to find the right road again. When all else fails, you can always follow the bus stops saying 'To City' or 'Out of City' (meaning Bridgetown) to help get your bearings. Driving is on the left, and cars are right-hand drive. All passengers must wear seat belts in the front and back seats, and the use of mobile phones is illegal while driving (except in 'hands-free' mode). The speed limit is 40 or 60 kph depending on the type of road; the ABC Highway and Mighty Grynner Highway (formerly Spring Garden Highway) and short sections of Highway 2A have an upper limit of 80 kph. There are plenty of fuel stations in and around Bridgetown, on the main highways and along the west and south coasts; there are fewer on the east coast but distances are very short.

Car hire To hire a car, drivers need to be 21, and those over 80 (or in some cases 75) must supply a medical certificate that shows they are fit to drive. You must have a valid (photo) driving licence from your own country of residence that has been valid for at least two years, and a credit card (even if you settle the bill in cash). Car hire is efficient and generally reliable and regular cars, Mini-Mokes, compact SUVs, jeeps and minibuses are all available. Rental companies will deliver

> **Tip...**
> There are more than 50 car-hire companies on Barbados but recommended for more than 40 years' experience, good service and fleet of 500 vehicles is Drive-A-Matic Car Rentals, Grantley Adams International Airport, T434 8440, www.carhire.tv, daily 0500-2300.

a vehicle to the airport, the cruise terminal or directly to hotels (and can arrange drop-off at a different location for no extra fee), provide a free road map of the island, and will also arrange a local driving permit (mandatory) at a cost of US$5 for two months or US$50 for one year. Many rental companies offer GPS/satnav systems as well as baby and child booster seats, and surfboard roof racks for an extra fee. A Mini-Moke or small car will cost around US$50-60 a day, a sedan/saloon or jeep US$60-80, and an SUV or small minibus US$80-100, with discounts for seven or more days. Basic hire generally only includes statutory third-party insurance; you are advised to take out the optional collision damage waiver premium at US$12-15 per day as even the smallest accident can be very expensive. All charges for car hire and extras are subject to VAT of 17.5%.

Taxi

All official taxis have licence plates denoted with a ZR; there are plenty of taxis at the airport, and any hotel and restaurant can phone one. They are unmetered and fares are regulated, but establish what the journey will cost before setting off. At the airport, there is a board displaying the standard taxi fares to various points on the island, which are also listed on the airport's website ⓘ *www.gaia.bb/content/taxi-rates-airport*. Sample fares from the airport are US$24 to Oistins, US$31 to St Lawrence Gap, US$46 to Bridgetown, US$58 to Holetown and US$73 to Speightstown for a car for four people (minibuses are also available). If you find a driver you like, get their card and phone number, and he/she may also offer to be your driver on a tour of the island. Always book ahead if you have a flight to catch. Barbados also has a ride-hailing taxi app, **pickUP** ⓘ *www.pickupbarbados.com*, that uses only officially registered drivers. You can pay by cash or credit card and schedule a ride for later in the day.

Essentials A-Z

Accidents and emergencies

Ambulance T511, **Fire** T311, **Police** T211. **Directory assistance** T411.

Customs and duty free

The duty-free alcohol allowance upon entry to Barbados is 1 litre of spirits or wine. It is permitted to bring up to 200 cigarettes or 100 cigars for personal use, but significant duty must be paid. Fresh fruit and vegetables, plants, cuttings and seeds are restricted or prohibited, depending on where they've come from, to prevent the transmission of pests and disease.

Travelling with a disability

Both the airport and Bridgetown Cruise Terminal have good accessibility for wheelchairs but they are not accommodated on public road transport and the towns have very uneven pavements. However, modern resorts and hotels have rooms with facilities for disabled travellers and many of the sites are accessible: for example, Nidhe Israel Synagogue and Museum, Mount Gay Rum Tour, the electric tram at Harrison's Cave, the trails at Welchman Hall Gully, Rochelle's Garden at the National Botanical Gardens, and South Coast Boardwalk. To watch cricket at Kensington Oval, all stands have ramped access and staff will assist. It's easy enough to tour the island in a taxi (a larger minivan for wheelchair storage), in a rented vehicle or by boat, and local people will do their very best to help.

Drugs

If you are offered drugs on the beach, in a rum shop or at a party, do not be tempted to dabble; all are illegal and law does not allow for 'personal possession'. Larger amounts of marijuana or any amount of cocaine will get you charged with trafficking and penalties are very severe.

Electricity

115 volts/50 cycles (similar to USA). Plug types are 2 flat blades or 2 flat blades with 1 round grounding pin. Some houses and hotels also have 240 volt sockets for use with British equipment or adaptors with 3 rectangular pins, but take your own, just in case.

Embassies and consulates

For all Barbados embassies and consulates abroad and for foreign embassies and consulates on Barbados, see http://embassy.goabroad.com.

Health

Travel on Barbados poses no health risk to the average visitor provided sensible precautions are taken. Make sure you have sufficient medical travel insurance, get a dental check, know your own blood group and, if you suffer from allergies, diabetes or epilepsy, add your emergency information to the lock screen of your mobile phone or obtain a **Medic Alert bracelet** (www.medicalert.org.uk). If you wear glasses, take a copy of your prescription. A yellow fever inoculation certificate must be produced on arrival if you have arrived within five days of leaving an area in Africa or South America affected with yellow fever.

Insect-borne risks

There are minor mosquito-borne disease risks in the Caribbean region; **dengue fever**, **chikungunya virus** (also known as chik V), and **Zika (ZIKV) virus**. Although the risk of contracting any of these is very low, it is always a good idea to protect yourself against mosquitoes; try to wear clothes that cover arms and legs at dusk and dawn (when mosquitoes are most active) and use effective mosquito repellent. Rooms with a/c or fans also help ward off mosquitoes at night.

Stomach issues

Some form of diarrhoea or intestinal upset may affect some holidaymakers. The standard advice is always to wash your hands before eating and to be careful with drinking water and ice. Tap water is generally very good, but if in any doubt buy bottled water. Food can also pose a problem; be wary of salads if you don't know whether they have been washed or not. Symptoms should be relatively short-lived. Adults can use an antidiarrhoeal medication to control the symptoms but only for up to 24 hrs. In addition, keep well hydrated by drinking plenty of fluids and eat bland foods. Rehydration sachets mixed with water are a useful way to keep well hydrated and should always be used when treating children and the elderly. If symptoms persist, consult a doctor.

Sun

The climate is hot, and do not be deceived by cooling sea breezes. Protect yourself adequately against the sun with high-factor sunscreen (greater than SPF15) and also make sure it screens against UVB. Prevent heat exhaustion and heatstroke by drinking enough fluids throughout the day (your urine will be pale if you are drinking enough). Symptoms of heat exhaustion and heatstroke include dizziness, tiredness and headache. Use rehydration sachets to replenish fluids and salts and find somewhere cool and shady to recover. If you suspect heatstroke rather than heat exhaustion, you need to cool the body down quickly (cold showers are particularly effective).

If you get sick

The two main hospitals on the island, both in Bridgetown, offer all services including 24 hr A&E departments and helicopter air ambulances. There are a number of other medical centres and clinics and the larger hotels have doctors on call. In the event of a diving emergency, the Barbados hyperbaric chamber is at the Barbados Defence Force Headquarters, St Ann's Fort, Bridgetown, T436 5483.

Bayview Hospital, St Paul's Av, off Bay St, T436 5446, www.bayviewhospital.com.bb.
Queen Elizabeth Hospital (QEH), Martindale's Rd, east of Fairchild Street Bus Terminal, T436 6450, www.qehconnect.com.

Useful websites

www.cdc.gov US government Centers for Disease Control and Prevention site that gives excellent advice on travel health and disease outbreaks.
www.gov.uk/foreign-travel-advice Foreign travel advice from the British government that has useful information on each country including security, health and a list of UK embassies/consulates.
www.fitfortravel.nhs.uk A-Z of vaccine/health advice for each country.
www.travelhealth.co.uk Independent travel health site with advice on preparation, travel insurance and health risks.
www.who.int World Health Organization, updates of disease outbreaks.

Insurance

Before departure, it is vital to take out comprehensive travel insurance. There are numerous policies to choose from, so shop around. At the very least, the policy should cover medical expenses, including repatriation to your home country in the event of a medical emergency. Hospital bills need to be paid at the time of admittance, so keep all paperwork to make a claim. There is no substitute for suitable precautions against petty crime, but if you do have something stolen, report the incident to the nearest police station and make sure you get a police report and case number (you will need these to make a claim).

Language

English is the official language although there is a Barbadian dialect spoken, which incorporates West African languages. Barbados uses British spelling of English.

LGBTQIA+ travellers

In 2022, same-sex intimacy was decriminalized, and plans to recognize same-sex civil unions are in the legal pipeline. Barbados held its first Pride Week in 2018 raising awareness and acceptance. There's a relaxed attitude in the tourism industry, although public displays of affection are ill-advised.

Money

US$1 = B$2; UK£1 = B$2.70; €1 = B$2.30 (October 2025).

The currency is the Barbadian or Bajan dollar, B$, which has been pegged at B$2=US$1 since 1975. Notes are B$2, 5, 10, 20, 50 and 100 and coins are B$1, 25 cents, 10 cents, 5 cents and 1 cent. Many hotels, airlines and tour operators quote in US dollars; if paying cash you will get any change in B$.

Changing money

The easiest currencies to exchange are US and Canadian dollars, UK pounds and euros. Credit, debit, and prepaid currency cards are widely accepted for purchases, and there are ATMs and foreign exchange bureaux at the airport, and plenty of banks and ATMs in Bridgetown and the other main towns. ATMs are also found in supermarkets, shopping centres and some fuel stations. Inform your bank before you travel that you are going to Barbados so they don't put a stop on your card, and bring contact details from home of who to call if your card is lost or stolen.

Opening hours

Banks open Mon-Thu 0800-1400, Fri 0800-1600. Banks at shopping centres are usually open Mon-Thu 0930-1530, Fri 0930-1600, and some open Sat 1000-1500.
Shops are generally open Mon-Fri 0900-1700, Sat 0900-1300, although the larger supermarkets like Massy Stores open until at least 1900 and on Sun too.

Post and courier services

The **General Post Office** is on Cheapside, Bridgetown, T535 3900, and there are district post offices in every parish, open Mon-Fri 0730-1700. For courier services, **DHL** ⓘ *www.dhl.com.bb*, and **Fedex** ⓘ *www.fedex.com* cover the island.

Public holidays

1 Jan   New Year's Day
21 Jan   Errol Barrow Day
Mar/Apr   Good Fri, Easter Mon
28 Apr   National Heroes' Day
1 May   Labour Day
May/Jun   Whit Mon
1 Aug   Emancipation Day
1st Mon in Aug   Kadooment Day
30 Nov   Independence Day
25 Dec   Christmas Day
26 Dec   Boxing Day

Safety

Most visits to Barbados are trouble-free, but there are isolated incidents of crime, including armed robbery, theft from vehicles and sexual assault. But Barbadians are, as a rule, exceptionally friendly, honest and ready to help, and most visitors will have a safe and enjoyable stay. The general common-sense rules apply to prevent petty theft: don't exhibit anything valuable and keep wallets and purses out of sight; do not leave your possessions unattended on the beach; use a hotel safe to store valuables; lock doors as noisy fans and a/c can provide cover for sneak thieves; don't leave items on balconies when you go out; at night, avoid deserted areas, including the beaches, and always take taxis. If hiring a car, don't stop if you're flagged down by pedestrians, keep valuables out of sight and lock car doors when driving.

Tax

Departure tax is included in the cost of the air ticket at the point of purchase. 17.5% VAT is included in all prices in shops, and in duty-free outlets both full and tax-free prices are usually denoted. In hotels, 10% hotel VAT and 10% service charge will be added to your bill, usually as a single charge of 20%. Additionally, room-rate levy (between US$4 and US$18 per night depending on the rate and accommodation class), which must be paid directly to the hotel. Be sure to check whether or not these costs have been included in final accommodation quotes. 17.5% VAT and a 2.5% product levy are included in restaurant menu prices, but most also automatically add a 10% service charge to the bill (sometimes 15% for tables of 10 or more).

Telephone and internet

The IDD code for Barbados is +246, followed by a 7-digit number. **Digicel** ⓘ *www.digicelgroup.com*, and **Flow** ⓘ *www.discoverflow.co*, are Caribbean-wide cellular and internet providers. If you don't want to use roaming, local SIM cards and start-up packs are available from US$5 or, if you have a compatible phone, eSIM apps like Airalo, Saily, GigSky, Maya and Roamless offer good deals on data-only packs. Cellular outlets are at the airport, major towns and shopping malls, and you can top up via phone or the websites. However, you may choose not to bother, given that almost all hotels and eateries have free Wi-Fi.

Time

Atlantic Standard Time, 4 hrs behind GMT, 1 hr ahead of EST.

Tipping

Tipping is not mandatory, given that a service charge is added to hotel and restaurant bills and taxi fares are set by the government and taxi associations. However, given that Barbados receives so many US visitors, a tipping culture is prevalent, so by all means tip if you want to show your appreciation for waiters, guides, drivers or cleaning staff who have gone the extra mile; 10% is about right for good service, and it will be most appreciated.

Visas

Visitors must have a passport valid for the duration of your stay (plus an additional six months for those requiring a visa) and adequate unused pages for stamps. Even though you may not always get asked for it, all travellers need to be able to produce a return or onward ticket, proof that they can support themselves during their stay (a credit card will suffice), and an address at which they will be staying (the hotel on your first night should be enough). Most visitors do not need a visa (including citizens of the USA, UK, EU, most Commonwealth countries, South Africa and the Caribbean), although the length of stay permitted varies from 28 days to 6 months. Those in transit or visiting from a cruise ship for less than 24 hrs don't need visas either, even if they are from countries that would otherwise require one. For full details and how to apply for a visa, see the **Ministry of Foreign Affairs and Foreign Trade** website, www.foreign.gov.bb.

Extending your initial entry stamp is possible (for US$50) by applying to the **Chief Immigration Officer** ⓘ *Immigration Department, Careenage House on the Wharf in Bridgetown, T535 4100, Mon-Fri 0830-1600*. Additionally, Barbados (like much of the Caribbean) has introduced a remote working visa called the **Barbados 12 Month Welcome Stamp** to attract digital nomads and lifestyle migrants (www.barbadoswelcomestamp.bb). To be eligible, you must earn at least US$50,000 per year.

Index

*Entries in **bold** refer to maps*

A

accidents and emergencies 112
accommodation 20
    all-inclusive options 80
    price codes 20
Accra Beach 76
Agapey Chocolate Factory 32
airport information 106
air travel 105
Andromeda Botanic Gardens 64
Animal Flower Cave 57
Arlington House Museum 53

B

Barbados Museum 36
Barbados National Armoury 39
Barbados National Cannon Collection 39
Barbados Turf Club 37
Barbados Wildlife Reserve 59
Barclays Park 63
Bath 66
Bathsheba 63
Batts Rock 44
Bay Street 34
Boatyard, The 34
Bonnet, Stede 71
Bottom Bay 70
Brandons Beach 44
Bridgetown 26, **28**, **38**
Bridgetown Duty Free 47
Bridgetown Fish Market 28
Brighton Beach 44
Broad Street 27
Brownes Beach 34
bus travel 109

C

Caribbean Wax Museum 27
car hire 110
Carlisle Bay 34
Carlisle Bay Marine Park 35
car travel 110
Cathedral Church of Saint Michael and All Angels 32
Cattlewash 63
Chalky Mount 63
Chalky Mount Potteries 63
Chamberlain Bridge 31
Charles Duncan O'Neal Bridge 32
Charles Fort 40
chattel houses 21
Cheapside Public Market 28
Cherry Tree Hill 58
Christ Church Parish Church 74
climate 12
Coco Hills Forest 51
Codrington College 66
Coleridge Street 34
Coles Cave 51
Cove Bay 58
Crane Beach 72
cricket 17, 29, 30
Cricket Legends of Barbados 29
Crop Over 16
customs and duty free 112

D

disabled travellers 112
diving 17
Dottin's Reef 49
Dover Beach 75
drink 23
drugs 112

E

electricity 112
embassies and consulates 112
Enterprise Beach 73

F

Farley Hill National Park 60
festivals 12
Flower Forest Botanical Gardens 52
Folkestone Marine Park and Museum 49
food 22
Foul Bay 73
Foursquare Rum Distillery 70

G

Garrison Historic Area 35
Garrison Savannah 35
Garrison Tunnels 37
George Washington House 37
Gibbes Beach 54
golf 17
Government House 33
Grenade Hall Forest and Signal Station 59
Gun Hill Signal Station 41

H

Hackleton's Cliff 64
Harbour Lights 34
Harrismith Beach 70
Harrison's Cave Eco-Adventure Park 51
Harry Bayley Observatory 40
Hastings 76
health 112
hiking 18
history 99
Holetown 47
horse racing 18
hotels 20
    all-inclusive options 80
    price codes 20
Hunte's Gardens 52

I

insurance 113

J

Jack-in-the-Box Gully 51

K

Kensington Oval 30
kitesurfing 19

L

Ladder Bay 57
language 114
LGBTQIA+ travellers 114
Limegrove Lifestyle Centre 47
listings 78
Little Bay 57
Little Good Harbour 55
Liv's Lookout 52
Long Bay 71
Long Pond 62

M

Main Guard 36
Mallalieu Motor Collection 77
Martin's Bay 65
Maxwell Beach 74
Miami Beach 73
Military Cemetery 40
money 114
Montefiore Fountain 34
Morgan Lewis Sugar Mill 59
Mount Gay Visitor Centre 44
Mount Hillaby 51
Mullins Beach 54
Museum of Parliament and National Heroes Gallery 31
music 102

N

National Botanical Gardens 41
National Heroes Square 30
Needhams Point Lighthouse 40
Nidhe Israel Synagogue and Museum 33

O

Oistins Fish Fry 74

Open Garden Programme 14
Open House Programme 18
opening hours 114
Orchid World see Tropical Garden Barbados

P

Paradise Beach 44
Parliament Buildings 31
Parlour 63
Paynes Bay 44
Pebbles Beach 34
Pico Teneriffe 58
polo 18
Port St Charles 55
post and courier services 114

Q

Queen's Park 32
Queen's Park House 33

R

Ragged Point 67
restaurants 24, 85
  price codes 20
River Bay 57
road travel 109
Rockley (Accra) Beach 76
rum 44, 70

S

safety 114
sailing 19
Sandy Lane 46
sea travel 107
Shark Hole 72
Six Men's Bay 55
snorkelling 17
Soup Bowl 63

Speightstown 53
Speightstown Mural 54
Spout 57
Spring Garden 57
St Andrew's Parish Church 62
St Ann's Fort 39
St George Parish Church 41
St James Parish Church 49
St John Parish Church 65
St Lawrence Anglican Church 75
St Lawrence Gap 75
St Nicholas Abbey 58
St Peter's Parish Church 54
Sunbury Plantation Great House 69
surfing 19
Swan Street 33

T

tax 115
taxis 111
telephone and internet 115
tipping 115
transport 105
Tropical Garden Barbados 42
Turners Hall Woods 62
turtles 45

V

visas 115

W

weather 12
Welches Beach 74
Welchman Hall Gully 50
windsurfing 19
Worthing Beach 75

Bradt Island Guides

Just some of the destinations in our range...

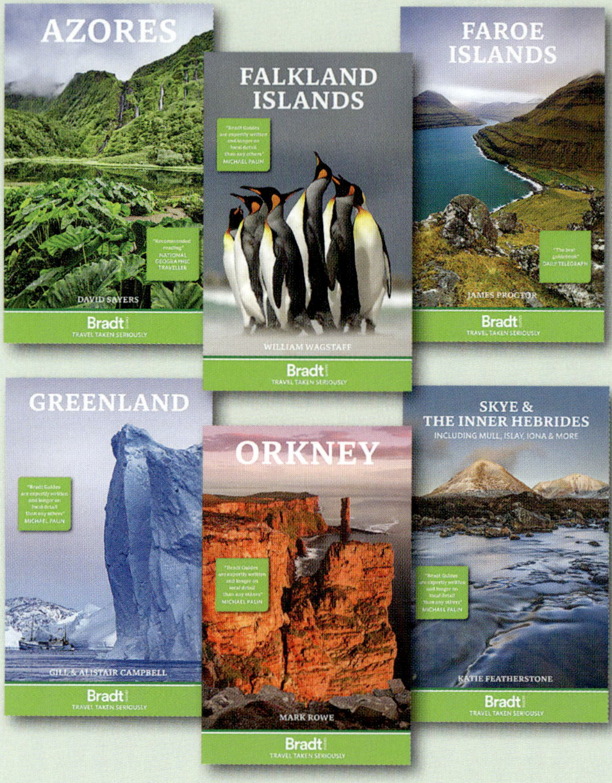

TRAVEL TAKEN SERIOUSLY

bradtguides.com/shop

 BradtGuides    @BradtGuides   @bradtguides

Features

All-inclusive options on Barbados 80
Barbados Railway 64
Beards and Bims – the naming of Barbados 40
Chattel houses 21
Crop Over 16
Flourishing gardens 14
Horsing around 37
Music 102
Oistins Fish Fry 74
Open House Programme 18
Sandy Lane 46
The Gentleman Pirate 71
The island 10
Turtles 45

Acknowledgements

The authors would like to thank Lizzie Williams, author of the previous edition, as well as those readers who have generously taken the time to contact us with updates, suggestions and corrections. We are very grateful in this regard to the following for their valuable contributions to the present edition: John Barrow, Lisa Best, Vickie Boswell, Margaret Bovell-Lewis, Andrew Clarke, Barry Collins, Kristy Condon, Jenny Dunstan, Ashley Elliott, Vince Fallon, Diana Farnen, Steve Fricke, Rachel Gabriella, Paul Gaskin, Katie Greenwood, Andrew Hardison, Savannah Harrison, Donna Hinds, Katey Holloway, Michael Howell, Nate Ingman, Jake Krall, Jeff Lawson, Peter Lowe, Dan MacWilliams, Natalie Matthews, Matt Morelli, Ann Morris, Christopher Nurse, David Oberhofer, Catherine O'Connor, Lynn Olmstead, John Popovich, Sabrina Rivers, Paige Thompson, Dave Watne, Shanna Wiand and Angela Worrell.

Special thanks are also due to all at Bradt Guides for their synergistic teamwork in bringing this edition to fruition with their trademark experience and efficiency.

Credits

Fifth edition published April 2026
Originally published by Footprint Handbooks and written by Sarah Cameron

Bradt Travel Guides Ltd
31a High Street, Chesham, Buckinghamshire, HP5 1BW, England
www.bradtguides.com
Print edition published in the USA by The Globe Pequot Press Inc, PO Box 480, Guilford, Connecticut 06437-0480

Text copyright © Bradt Travel Guides Ltd, 2026
Maps copyright © Bradt Travel Guides Ltd & Compass Maps 2026; includes map data
© OpenStreetMap contributors
Photographs copyright © Individual photographers, 2026 (see below)
Project Managers: Susannah Lord & BBR Design
Cover research: Pepi Bluck, Perfect Picture

Thank you for buying an authorized edition of this book published by Bradt Travel Guides. For over 50 years, Bradt Travel Guides has encouraged adventurous, immersive and responsible travel, and this is only possible because of the support of our readers. By purchasing our books, you are enabling us to continue to commission expert authors who genuinely know and love the places they write about, and who write their books after thorough, on-the-ground research.
The author and publisher have made every effort to ensure the accuracy of the information in this book at the time of going to press. However, they cannot accept any responsibility for loss, injury or inconvenience resulting from the use of information contained in this guide. All rights reserved. No part of this book may be reproduced, scanned or distributed by any means without the written permission of Bradt Travel Guides, nor used or reproduced in any way to train artificial intelligence technologies/ models. Bradt Travel Guides and the author unequivocally reserve this work from the text and data mining exception, as per Article 4(3) of the Digital Single Market Directive 2019/790.

ISBN: 9781804693612

British Library Cataloguing in Publication Data
A catalogue record for this book is available from the British Library

Importer to the EU: Freytag-Berndt u. Artaria KG, Ölzeltgasse 3/10, 1030 Wien, Österreich

Photographs
Front cover Bottom Bay Beach at dawn (Marco Arduino/4Corners)
Back cover Tropical flowers, Flower Forest Botanical Gardens (Giongi/Shutterstock.com); a traditional chattel house (Atosan/Shutterstock.com)
Inside front cover Chattel houses (zstock/Shutterstock.com); sea turtle (Giongi/Shutterstock.com); surfing (Otto Borik/Shutterstock.com)
Title page Worthing Beach (SHOWME Caribbean/Shutterstock.com)
Colour section pages 2-3: Orietta Gaspari/iStock.com; page 4: B Coster/Shutterstock.com, alfotokunst/ Shutterstock.com; page 5: Giongi/Shutterstock.com, SimplyAdrienne/Shutterstock.com, Simon Dannhauer/ Shutterstock.com; page 7: Filip Fuxa/Shutterstock.com, Alan Copson/AWL Images.

Maps David McCutcheon FBCart.S. FRGS, assisted by Pearl Geo Solutions
Typeset by BBR Design
Production managed by Imprint Press; printed in India
Digital conversion by www.dataworks.co.in